PARENTS AND

PARTNERS IN LEARNING

TEACHERS

PARENTS AND
PARTNERS IN LEARNING
TEACHERS

JANE BASKWILL

SCHOLASTIC
Toronto • Sydney • New York • London • Auckland

Scholastic-TAB Publications Ltd.
123 Newkirk Road, Richmond Hill, Ontario, Canada L4C 3G5

Scholastic Inc.
730 Broadway, New York, NY 10003, USA

Ashton Scholastic Limited
165 Marua Road, Panmure, PO Box 12328, Auckland 6, New Zealand

Ashton Scholastic Pty Limited
PO Box 579, Gosford, NSW, 2250, Australia

Scholastic Publications Ltd.
Holly Walk, Leamington Spa, Warwickshire CV32 4LS, England

Cover by Adriana Taddeo

Canadian Cataloguing in Publication Data

Baskwill, Jane

Parents and teachers: partners in learning

Includes bibliographical references

ISBN 0-590-73187-4

1. Parent-teacher relationships. 2. Education —
Parent participation. Education of children.
I. Title.

LC225.B38 1989   371.1'03   C89-094915-8

6 5 4 3 2 1   Printed in Canada   9/8 0 1 2 3 4 5/9

*To my first families, who began the whole process:
the Smiths, Townsends, Rockwells and Sutherlands
in Canning, Nova Scotia.*

*The names of the individuals participating
in my research have been changed,
but they know who they are,
and to each of them I owe a debt of gratitude.*

Contents

Turning tears into smiles

I looked across at Carol's mother, her tired, dejected face now streaming with tears, and asked myself how much she really understood about literacy development. Did she even yet grasp the reason why her daughter would have to remain another year in the same class? What message had I given her that made her feel both she and Carol were failures? Hadn't I made it clear that her daughter wouldn't be "repeating" a year, just continuing from where she'd left off so she could gain the confidence she needed without the frustration she might experience if she were moved ahead too soon? Had my explanation of what her child could already do, and what she would learn to do over the course of the following year, really been so inadequate?

As I accompanied the still tearful woman to the door she said, "I know you'll do the best for Carol. I trust you."

Instead of being overjoyed by this display of blind trust and confidence I felt uneasy, burdened by the implications. This parent was putting complete faith in what seemed to her the all-powerful healing abilities of the school, particularly of me, the teacher. And implicit in that trust was no recognition at all that effective help also lay within the confines and abilities of her home. Her sense of personal failure was pronounced, as was her feeling that any possible remedy was totally up to the school. She saw her child's successes as insignificant in the overall scheme of passing and failing. She was comparing Carol with other children, without recognizing her own continuing role in the child's literacy development.

The notion that teaching and learning are unique attributes of school, nurturing the unique attribute of home, has fostered separate, rigidly set lists of responsibilities that create an ever-widening communication gap between home and school. And as teachers know only too well, when communication between home and school breaks down, it's they who ultimately bear the brunt of the concerns or complaints — and they, usually, who are expected to provide the remedies.

I've discovered in talking to adults about their school experiences that many of their memories are tinged with disappointment, regret, even bitterness. School they recall as something they endured. Many feel that what they were expected to learn bore little relationship to their real interests or talents. Packaged knowledge was doled out to them like medicine, in precise doses, not for their enjoyment but "for their own good." The dismal picture these people still carry of their own schooling colors and distorts their perceptions of how their children learn and what they, as parents, can do to support that learning. It affects how they interpret information they receive from the school and how they respond to it.

Meanwhile, the old belief that there is an optimum time when particular facets of learning can most successfully occur has changed. In the past 20 years an increasing number of researchers have been taking a closer look at how language and literacy develop in young children. Their writings have focused on the nature of the home environment, where children are inspired to master such complex tasks as walking and talking, and even reading and writing, with apparent ease — and without instruction in the formal sense (Clark, 1976; Doake, 1981; Harste, Burke and Woodward, 1984; Holdaway, 1979; Newman, 1984; Taylor, 1984). Teachers are now adding their voices as well, describing how they have translated research into classroom practice (Atwell, 1987; Baskwill and Whitman, 1986; Hansen, Newkirk and Graves, 1985; Newkirk and Atwell, 1982; Newman, 1985). Out of that research, and through the voices of those teachers, has developed a picture of what the school learning environment ought to be.

A philosophy of learning known as "whole language" has emerged, based on the belief that children enter school as already experienced learners and that their need and desire to learn will grow and prosper within a safe and supportive environment, where they are surrounded by quality materials, where they see others engaged in the same tasks, and where they have time for self-initiated practice. Because this picture grows out of the home, not in competition with it, the children's learning and well-being become the shared responsibility of both parents and teacher. And fluent communication between the two becomes vital.

In the past I felt comfortable communicating with parents in what I thought was the lingua franca of grades, marks, readiness skills, passing and failing. With that kind of evaluation system there was really little left for me to say — and little asked of me. But now that I'm a whole language teacher that's no longer the case. My new beliefs about how children learn, and my growing observations of that learning in progress, can't be effectively communicated in that terribly limited

3

language. I need another language — one that's new to me but even more so to parents who are unaccustomed to hearing their children talked about in such a way. Most scarcely even recognize the new world of learning, since it differs so drastically from the one they remember.

In the last few years I've come to value highly the many things parents have taught me. For one thing, I've learned to free myself from pedagogical jargon and talk more clearly about what I'm doing in the classroom. I've learned to recognize the questions behind the questions parents ask, and to refrain from jumping to conclusions about what they really mean. I've learned not to make assumptions about what parents will or won't want, what they will or won't like. Most of all, I've learned to take pleasure in small advances and not to expect growth in mutual understanding to occur overnight.

In the following pages I describe my developing awareness of the communication gap between me and my students' parents, the profound change in my thinking, and the course of action I took in my effort to reshape the traditional teacher/parent communication model. I include comments from parents, transcribed from home interviews, dialogue journals, notes and the informal meetings I held throughout each school year. These comments reflect the changes that occurred in my relationship with those parents, and describe the mutual support that developed between us. I hope you'll find that some of these ideas and reflections are useful as you develop your own ways for you and your students' parents to forge a successful partnership in the education of their children.

Parents have given me a great deal over the years and I hope I can, through you, give something back to them. After all, they shared their children with me — a gift not easily repaid!

Reaching out to parents

My meeting with Carol's mother, and with others like her, made me think seriously about my relationship with parents. Whether we realize it or not, we teachers have a great deal of power over the lives not only of the children we teach but of their families as well. We have the power to make the best of parents doubt their own abilities. We have the power to create feelings of guilt or frustration, to confuse, anger or reduce to tears even the most stalwart. We have the power to impose — or simply allow — an unbalanced relationship that puts too much guilt on one party, too much authority and responsibility on the other, so that no real communication, no real sharing of ideas and information can occur. The problem is how to prevent that kind of imbalance, how to ensure shared understanding and joint goals.

I had been making what seemed to me reasonable efforts to reach the parents and keep them informed about their children's progress. I had been available for parent/teacher conferences, had attended home and school nights, had written anecdotal comments on report cards. Why hadn't my efforts been getting results? Why were the parent/teacher meetings I arranged so sparsely attended? Weren't the parents interested? Or, like Carol's mother, did they simply not understand? I began to wonder if communicating with parents was an impossible task.

I tried a parent volunteer program, hoping it would at least get the parents into the school. It didn't. The few volunteers who came usually did their assigned tasks for the day and left before I had time to talk to them about anything else. I had no way of knowing what their impressions were of my classroom or what they might be saying about it to the community at large. I thought of it as a happy place, but if they were so anxious to leave, could it be that it felt cold and forbidding to them?

As my frustration continued to mount, so did my sense of guilt. I began to think about the parents' point of view: what was I doing to encourage the reluctant or the awkward, and what could I learn from those who were already doing their best to communicate with me? The more I thought about it, the more my conviction grew that it was my responsibility to improve the situation. I knew, of course, that difficulty communicating with parents wasn't something new or peculiar to me. Furthermore, I recognized that my failure to communicate with them was mirrored in their inability or reluctance, whatever the reason, to communicate with me. I was the one with a global view of how home and school interrelate, and it was my role to help them understand and benefit from our relationship.

I had read numerous articles calling for teachers to communicate more effectively with parents. I was hearing catch-phrases like "Parents As Partners," "P.A.L." (Parent Assisted Learning), "Parents Are a Child's First Teacher," and "Parents Make the Difference" at teacher workshops. I even knew of several government-funded projects set up to inform parents, most often targeted at those whose children were having reading problems. But I hadn't found any information about effective alternatives to the workshop/meeting model of parent/teacher communication — and that obviously wasn't the answer. For one thing, such meetings were too formal. They made communication between home and school something special rather than a natural and expected sharing of information and responsibility.

At the same time I'd begun to realize that the problem went even deeper than I had imagined. It was inevitable that their own school experiences would color parents' expectations of my classroom and my methods. I found it hard to believe they might be upset or confused about what I was doing, but could that be part of the problem? How could I expect them to share my understanding of such new terms as whole language, predictable books, big books, shared language, independent practice, and personal writing? Had I been trying too hard to communicate specifics that made no sense to parents who trusted me but didn't understand what I was trying to do?

I decided to listen much more closely to parents, not just to the parents of my students, but to friends who were parents, to parents at workshops and to parents who were teachers themselves. Everywhere I went I listened — in the bank, in the post office, at the pool, in the grocery store — as they spoke about their children's teachers and schools. My conclusion was so ironically simple that it amazed me: the problem with parent/teacher communication was that there was none! There was no effective and continuous two-way communication that would allow the mutual insight and sharing my instincts had been craving.

In a grocery store, my shopping cart like a shield between us, I struck up a conversation with a parent whose child would be entering my class that Fall.

"I wonder how he'll like it?" I ventured.

7

"I don't expect he will, but he'll get used to it," she replied.

"What makes you say that?"

"Oh, I expect it hasn't changed much since I was there," she offered. "He doesn't sit still very long, and he still can't color in the lines. He knows all his colors, though. I've been working on his printing, but he just won't pay attention — I can't get him to stay at it very long. I told him he's going to have to change when he gets in school or he won't grade."

How revealing! She had never even been in my classroom, but she thought she had a clear picture of it in her mind — or at least of its implications. I thought of it as a warm, friendly place, not unlike home. She thought of it as cold and rigid, a place full of rules and standards against which her child would be measured. She imagined failure before the child had even set foot in the door!

Yet this same parent had created a warm, supportive home that had encouraged his efforts to learn how to talk and walk. Don Holdaway has addressed this incongruity:

> It is astonishing that the same parents who supported their child's learning of speech with such good sense so often act in a completely opposite and destructive manner when the child begins to have difficulties reading and writing. Of course, we must accept that they learned to act in such a way from their own schooling, and that probably, as teachers, much of what we [his emphasis] do in teaching stems from the same sources. (Holdaway, 1979, p.189)

I strongly believe that literacy will develop naturally within a genuine context embedded in a safe, supportive environment. I have faith that children will learn to read and write as readily as they learned to walk and talk if there are quality materials available, constant models of adults and other children engaged in the tasks, and ample opportunity for self-directed practice. Most parents, on the other hand, believe that school learning must be divided into small bits to be mastered in a sequential order. They dread failure but expect it in a sink-or-swim, everyone-for-number-one environment. School is not a place to be enjoyed. And from their own school days they remember that parental contact with the school almost invariably means a child in trouble.

For generations parents and teachers have been stuck in that self-perpetuating paradigm. What we need is a shift in thinking about the nature of effective home/school communication, a new model of reciprocal responsibility based on a mutual understanding of what learning is. I began to dream of teachers communicating with parents on a regular basis, sharing everything they noticed about their children's growth in learning. Indeed, even more important, I imagined parents doing the same with teachers, feeling it was their place — and their right — to do so. I knew that somehow we had to make sure teachers and parents were on the same wave length to begin with, and then encourage them to set up an appropriate method and means of regular communication.

But how could we be sure that true communication would result? Parents draw on a wide variety of experiences, and much of what they know and believe about learning, and about their children's school experiences, is based on their own past. How could we meet such varied needs? How could we help parents share our own picture of a whole language classroom? How could we encourage them to support their children's school learning in the same natural way they supported their preschool learning? How could we open a two-way line of communication, one that would not only inform but also provide mutual support?

Then, one evening as I sat at my dining room table writing notes to family and friends, it occurred to me that the kind of contact found among family members might be the very one I'd been searching for in my dealings with parents: a reciprocal communication that would occur naturally. In families, every member has certain expectations of the others: we expect them to keep in touch with us via mail, telephone, visits or messages from mutual friends, and they expect the same from us. We expect them to share day-to-day information and anecdotes about themselves and their children. We expect them to be open about their feelings and feel comfortable about probing ours. We expect mutual trust.

Using the family model dramatically changes the picture of a teacher/parent relationship. It becomes a relationship built on trust and understanding, one in which communication prospers, confrontation and blame disappear. It frees thinking and opens the way to a more frequent, more useful, more comfortable sharing of home and school experiences.

Changing attitudes

I had periodically received phone calls or notes from parents, mostly initiated by them and requiring little, if any, response from me. Why had I never bothered to initiate a friendly written exchange? I seldom simply dropped a parent a line just to keep in touch, and I almost never initiated a telephone conversation. Most of my face-to-face contact was during parent/teacher conferences or following special events like the Christmas concert, usually very brief and very formal conversations.

But now I saw other possibilities. I could encourage parents to write to me by writing to them. I could write to a worried parent about her child's day. I could write to the parents of a child with a cold to say how he had been. I could write Carl's mom about the letter he wrote during personal writing, so she could look for it and help him mail it. I could write to Tess's dad about the book Tess was reading during practice time, and perhaps encourage him to let her buy her own copy next time the book orders were sent. I could try the dialogue journal David Doake had been after me to try. These notebooks, which travel back and forth between home and school, would give the parents a place to jot down their questions or reflections, and me an opportunity to respond to those questions and concerns in greater detail.

I could also use the telephone more often to keep in touch with working parents, or with parents who were otherwise unable to get to the school. I could take a minute to chat with parents who came to pick up their children for doctor's appointments, look for lost clothing or bring forgotten lunch boxes, if only to share a recent anecdote or report some success or achievement that involved their children. Positive news would surely encourage them to return to the school and perhaps entice them to stay once they were there.

Since bookstores in our area are few and far between, I began to think about ways to share some of my own and my school's books with parents — not only good children's books but also some excellent ones on how to do crafts, how to spend quality time with children, how to handle temper tantrums or thumb-sucking, how to keep a rainy day or a birthday party manageable — skills I'm continuing to acquire myself as my own family grows up. Perhaps the pressure parents often feel would be reduced if they saw that their problems were really quite common after all. I thought about a lending library where books of this nature would travel back and forth from school to home. With my new family model in place it felt right and perfectly natural to share with parents the books I had enjoyed and, in turn, be open myself to their reading recommendations.

And there had to be a way of making meetings more enticing and interesting. I could offer a variety of workshops, not just meetings dealing directly with the children's progress, but also informative ones about education in general. I even planned to devise ways of having parents and children actively participate in workshops together. I wanted to work on giving my parents a more accurate picture of what my class was like every day. Perhaps a booklet and a slide presentation would help by providing a common basis for discussion and pointing out natural home/school links.

My head was buzzing with the possibilities of working toward a reciprocal communication model. The key lay first and foremost in changing my own thinking, but I had made a reasonably good start there. Now, freed from the traditional model, I was limited only by my own time and energy. I realized that other teachers had tried some of the projects I was planning to try, but in a different way — usually directed at parents in a one-way communication designed to impart information in a way convenient for them. They discouraged responses; an acknowledgement, brief and simple, was all they generally required or desired. There was no room for interaction, let alone any opportunity for the parent to develop control over the activity. As you will see in the more detailed descriptions that follow, ownership of my projects became joint as parents incorporated the activities into their home life styles.

The nature of each project ensured that it would provide a working example of functioning reciprocal communication. I provided the initiative by beginning a particular form of communication: sending a note or a bag of books, or writing the first entry in a dialogue journal. This was an invitation to the parent to participate. In due course, as the parents began to feel comfortable and respond, they assumed control of that mode of communication and made it their own.

I encourage the children in my whole language classroom to take risks and engage in independent learning, and provide safety nets which allow them to do so. I provided similar safety nets for the parents so they knew that the risks they took would to be accepted and encouraged. Sometimes they didn't pick up on a particular invitation right away; some preferred one form of communication over another. That was fine. I no longer felt I had to have the same kind or amount of communication with everyone — I knew that now I would have some communication with all families. Even so, when I look back I realize that at the time I never understood the full implications of all that was possible.

In the rest of the book you'll find not only descriptions of the projects I tried, but also some of the parents' reactions, through quotations from interviews, journals and notes. It may seem overwhelming if you picture all these projects in place at one time; I wouldn't suggest that you try them all at once. However I did discover that the more I did, and the more ways I did each one, the more response I got from more parents. I also found that once a particular project was established and working, sustaining and improving it became relatively simple.

One other thing I learned is not to be discouraged if only one parent comes to a workshop, or if only eight respond in their dialogue journals. I rejoice in whatever participation I find; the response of only one parent is quite enough to inspire me not only to persevere, but to redouble my efforts to make my approach even more welcoming.

The biggest change has been in my attitude and in my understanding of what constitutes a reciprocal communication relationship. Without that change these projects would have been no more effective than what I was doing before. I can now say with conviction that if you are prepared to change your own attitude you'll find that parents will welcome the change and respond with warmth and enthusiasm.

Inviting participation

Communicating with parents requires a variety of projects from which they can pick and choose whatever they find useful or interesting, and my aim was to find some form of communication that would appeal to every parent.

Parent survey

Literacy values — that is, the importance parents place on reading and writing in their own lives and those of their children — obviously vary from home to home. Yet all parents support their children while they are learning the equally arduous tasks of walking and talking, and that support will naturally extend to literacy pursuits *unless parents are made to feel that their self-worth or cultural heritage is being undermined.*

I discovered that what I thought I knew about the families of my students and the literacy in their homes was based mostly on assumptions rather than direct information. I wanted to know more, especially about their reading habits and their understanding of, and attitude toward, learning. I needed to discover what picture of school they had in their minds, and share a little of the picture I had in mine.

Appendix A (page 72) shows the survey I began to use with parents of incoming children at our annual preschool registration. Normally registration included a simple assessment of the children's knowledge of letters and numerals, and their recognition of shape and color, as well as a health history supplied by the parents. Not surprisingly, considering their own school memories, parents often seemed as nervous as the children at this first encounter with school. So my survey tried to shift the focus away from what the children knew to what had been happening in the home up to that point. My purpose was to signal to the parents the shift in my thinking and to alert them to the vital importance of their own role and the respect I would accord it. The survey was easy to use: I simply wrote down the parents' oral answers while their children busied themselves with books, paper and writing implements.

Each year I learn more interesting things from the survey, and eventually I hope to see a change in the pattern of responses. Here, for example, are some of the things I discovered the first year I conducted the survey:

- In 20 out of 24 families the children weren't read to on a daily basis.

- They were read to, on average, about four times a week, usually just before bedtime.

- Those families who did make a regular daily practice of reading to the children read to them throughout the day as well as at bedtime.

- Nineteen of the 24 parents didn't consider themselves good readers who read for pleasure.

- They couldn't remember how they learned to read, simply claiming it was "in school." They didn't consider their own parents good readers either.

- The five good readers could all remember being read to in the home, and could recall examples of particular story favorites.

- All 24 felt that reading is an important and necessary life skill.

- All believed a good reader to be one who makes sense of what he or she is reading.

- All 24 parents acknowledged their children's love for stories.

This survey constituted my first dialogue with parents. I didn't use its results to make a list of at-risk children, or to group them according to need. I was now thinking of my parents as partners in the reading process, and I didn't want any hidden agendas or unrealistic expectations. If they were willing, I would simply provide them with the model, the materials and the opportunities for self-initiated practice.

Through the survey I had gained a fuller understanding of the nature of the children's home encounters with print, and of the parents' attitudes towards those experiences. But I knew I must hold that understanding in confidence and not subject it to judgment; I was no longer tempted to follow up by lecturing families on the merits of reading to children or by enrolling them or their children in special summer workshops. I wanted to make sure they wouldn't become guarded in their responses, or not show up at future interviews because they felt I'd betrayed their trust.

I have often been asked if parents object to or feel uncomfortable answering my survey questions. So far that has never been the case, nor has any parent refused to answer, so the survey has become a normal part of my preschool registration routine. However I have had to work hard at making parents feel comfortable with the interview itself, while at the same time ensuring that their responses would be genuine. Over the years my technique has improved, but the first year I simply explained that I was trying something new and asked them to bear with me as we worked our way through the questions. They may well have wondered what I was doing, some may even have questioned my sanity, but none has ever questioned my sincerity.

Parent booklet

I realized that some of the communication problems I'd experienced in the past had come about because parents didn't feel at ease talking with me, with other parents, or even with their own children about what was happening in my classroom. Many parents feel upset when their children say "played" or "nothing" in response to the question, "What did you do in school today?" I wanted to give them the language they needed to talk about their children's day in terms the children would understand: in other words, in terms of the classroom. I decided, therefore, to put together a short booklet outlining each element of my program (see Appendix B, page 73). It would describe what the children might be doing, what I might be doing, the purpose of what we were doing, and when in the course of the day we would be doing it. The booklet had an attractive cover and a coil binding, since the school had a binding machine. It was a striking and professional looking production, but I could have produced a similar effect with a simpler stapled booklet.

At our first home/school meeting in September, I explained the various elements of the program and pointed out where in the classroom the activities took place. Then I distributed the booklet for the parents to take home. Familiarizing them with the language their children are accustomed to in the classroom allows them to discuss what's going on there in terms they are both familiar with. I wanted the parents to become insiders and confident participants. I wanted to wipe out the feeling so many have that they are no longer able to keep up with the changes taking place in modern schools.

As I had hoped, the parents began to direct their questions to a specific part of the day: "What did you do during shared language time today?" or "What area did you work in during independent practice?" Alicia's father said to me later: "I never realized you would talk like this to the children. I thought this was just a lot of jargon . . . but now I see that it was a big help because Alicia knew just what I was talking about when I used the terms she was familiar with."

But as well as making parents feel comfortable with their children's classroom and routine, the parent booklet offered other unexpected uses and benefits. I discovered that copies were ending up in the homes of preschoolers' parents. As Marcie's mom commented when she brought Marcie to register: "I feel as though I know what Marcie will be doing already. I can't wait for her to start—I know she'll have fun! Cinthea Lewis gave me the booklet you gave her where you describe how your program works. Dan and I have talked about it already, and it seems like a good idea to us."

Word was getting around! Parents were talking to each other about their children's first year in school and seemed to be helping each other adapt to the new words being used to describe their children's classroom and learning. Parents were becoming comfortable using such terms as personal writing, shared language and independent practice. At the same time they were becoming knowledgeable about how these activities worked and why they were included in the program. Naming provides a starting point for discussion. This booklet opened that door for parents and, through discussion, they were better able to sort out their questions and discover answers to them.

19

By giving parents the language of the classroom you empower them to talk about what goes on within the classroom in terms their children will respond to. You turn them from hesitant and apprehensive outsiders into confident participants fully able to keep up with the changes taking place within the school.

Notes

I made up my mind to write a brief note to several parents each day. I got in the habit of writing them throughout the day as significant events occurred, or at the end of classes while waiting for the school buses. I made sure the children knew what the notes were about; I usually wrote with the children sitting beside me and explained why I thought their parents would be interested:

◆ You've been using lots of beginning and ending letters when you're writing. I think your mom and dad should know so they'll be able to read your stories more easily.

◆ You didn't seem to be feeling well today. I'm going to mention this to Grammie so she'll tell Mom when she comes to pick you up tonight.

◆ You noticed many interesting things about The Owl and the Pussycat during shared language time today. I thought I'd share them with your dad.

Such comments made the children aware of what was going on, put my writing into a meaningful context and helped ensure that the note would be delivered. Soon the abundance of positive messages going home caused similar messages to come my way. Tacked on to the usual permission slips or excuse notes were:

◆ Charles has been writing me lovely stories with complete sentences and very "real" spellings lately. Illustrations are also terrific! (Mrs. Thomas)

◆ Marie was very proud of the plane she made during woodworking yesterday. She gave it to Robert and he was very happy with it. (Mrs. Carr)

Notes even began to appear at unexpected times:

◆ Hi! Hope you're having a good day. I asked Roger to give you this pick-me-up note with a piece of his birthday cake at noon. Hope you enjoy it! (Mrs. Wick)

My memos and notices also began to take on a new and more appealing look, with a computer graphic or hand-drawn illustration accompanying each message. I always read the notices to the children so they would know what they were about and consider safe delivery their responsibility. Should a note be lost along the way, they might even remember enough of it to tell their parents its contents and return with the requested materials or signatures anyway. The parents were amazed at the degree of responsibility their children demonstrated:

◆ I should have known John was right! He said he lost his note and that he needed a costume for his teddy bear for the Hallowe'en party. I thought I would just phone and check . . . I should have known! (Mrs. Marsh)

◆ As soon as Jennie comes home with a note she has me sit right down and then she reads it to me! (Mrs. Brock)

◆ Christopher brought two notes home the other day; one from you and one from the office, I think. He handed me the one from you and said: This is the important one, Mom! (Mrs. Collins)

Notes, memos and notices provide an easy way for parents and teachers to communicate with one another. As vehicles for communication, notes have long been part of the world of school, but the change in tone to a positive and sharing one will help parents and teachers use these avenues comfortably and to maximum benefit.

Dialogue journals

I knew a bit about dialogue journals — conversations in writing — but I didn't feel I was particularly successful with the few attempts I'd made to dialogue with my students. Then David Doake suggested using them with parents. "Oh no," I thought, "I could never do that." It would be risky to try with parents something I wasn't even good at with children. And I was convinced, in any case, that the parents would never bother to reply.

I'm not sure just what changed my mind. Perhaps it was the stack of old unused exam booklets I got at a local flea market one summer — an inexpensive resource with a reasonable number of pages. They stared at me, and by fall I'd decided to try journals. Because I wanted to make sure that everyone would understand how to use them and, more important, why we were using them, I handed them to the parents in person whenever possible.

I handed out what I could at a parent/teacher meeting early in the Fall and the remainder whenever the parents happened to come to the school. As a last resort, those I couldn't hand out personally I sent home with the children. In that case I included a short explanation of the purpose of the journal and a brief observation about the child. Appendix C (page 78) shows a sample of the covering letter to parents. I tried to encourage them to write, but I also made it clear that it wasn't mandatory and that neither I nor they would be interested in the other's handwriting or spelling skills!

I could have put an initial entry into each journal just to get things started, but I decided not to. I felt that the parents and I needed some time to get used to the whole idea and to experiment with how we wanted to use the journals. Besides being time-consuming, making entries for everyone could have appeared contrived and I didn't want parents to feel there was any hidden agenda. I knew there was no formula for successful dialogue journals with parents; I would just have to sit back and see what would happen.

About two weeks later the first journals began to arrive back with the children. I needn't have worried. The parents had written about things they'd noticed their children doing and saying: bits of conversation about school or a book, or something they had noticed the children writing. Out of a total of 24 families I ended up with eight regular correspondents and four who used the journal when they wanted more information or needed questions answered.

The journals are the property of the parents and I treat them as confidential, even though at times I get so excited by an entry I wish I could read it to other staff members. If I do decide to share an entry I'm always careful to ask permission first, and if the parent is the least bit hesitant I never press the issue. It's important for parents to trust that their entries will remain a private dialogue between parent and teacher; only then will they have the confidence to be honest and open about what is really on their minds.

I try to respond to each entry as clearly and concisely as possible, striving to maintain the tone of a friendly letter, as if I were writing to another family member. I found I improved with practice, so now my entries are much easier to write and take far less time.

With the writers' permission, I'd like to share a few sample journal entries and my responses to them:

November 24

Charles really enjoys stories. He especially enjoys reading a book — after I have read it to him — to his younger brother [three years old]. He has been pointing out the differences between the pictures and the story.

I find that he will practically memorize a book the first time I read it — especially if it includes a catchy song or jingle.

Very enthusiastic about book repairs and organization of bookshelf — airplane books together, circus books, etc. I think he reads from the pictures but seems to associate that a page with a lot of words takes longer so he talks more than when he reads a page with fewer words.

My reply:

November 26

Yes, Charles is getting quite "print-wise"! He is quick to remember a story, which frees him to practice matching his finger with his voice as he reads. By talking longer when he reaches a page with a lot of print he is showing that he understands how print works.

Most of the time my journal replies support the parents' observations; I've often found the observations they make about their children's reading and writing development very sensitive and detailed. Through my responses I try to confirm what they've observed and indicate what it means to me.

September 16

Tonight Sandy and her father drew an animal dot-to-dot. Upon completion, Dan asked her what it was and she said it was a pig. "How do you know?" "Because it has two eyes and a snort!" Sandy replied.

September 17

Gail decided to read Sandy a book from her school Berenstain Bear book bag. While Gail read the one about Too Much TV aloud, Sandy sat next to her on the couch with The Berenstain Bears Go to Camp. As she slowly turned the pages, Sandy pointed to the pictures and "read" aloud to herself. I think she was imitating her older sister and I think it's a good sign of her interest in learning to read. I would be interested to know what you think about it. What suggestions would you make?

My reply:

September 20

I think you are right about Sandy reading as she sees her older sister do. The hardest part usually is getting the older sibling to support this kind of activity rather than making fun or saying the child isn't really reading. You might keep this in mind and be on the lookout for such responses. I had to talk to Amanda about what it was like when she was learning to read and would get impatient with Nicholas.

When you or Dan read to Sandy, try to choose at least one story with which she's very familiar and invite her to read along. If the sentence reads "The fox went into the henhouse," you might pause after "the," encouraging her to chime in and finish it. As long as the word she supplies makes sense in the context of the story, don't worry if it's "cabin" for "hut," "puppy" for "dog." Only when it doesn't make sense should you gently wonder about it and see what else it might be.

As Sandy builds up a collection of familiar stories, these can be put in her bedroom or on a special shelf for her to read on her own — maybe before bed and after you have read to her. This is one way to support her growing interest gently and at the same time to demonstrate to her her own growing abilities. She will gain confidence in what she is able to do on her own. Keep me posted on how things are going.

Sometimes parents don't have a problem; they simply want to ask your opinion or advice. At other times there may be an actual concern, something they've been stewing over or brooding about but haven't been able to talk about. The following entry isn't the usual kind, since my reply required more time and careful thought than usual. However, it demonstrates the kind of concerns parents have and the way the dialogue journal allows these concerns to be aired positively and constructively.

March 2

I just came across this book again and decided to address a concern I have over Carl's writing.

He is very interested in communicating on paper and uses every opportunity at home to write letters to people — maybe just a note and/or picture for his sister, or perhaps a letter for a relative who lives far away. However he seems to have little concept of the actual construction of a letter as far as spacing words goes or writing from left to right until a line is filled, writing in a straight line and not seeming to know when to use capital or small letters. I have also noticed that he has difficulty writing down his numbers. Shouldn't he be learning these basic skills at this level to give him the groundwork he will need later on, or is it that these things are being taught but he hasn't absorbed them yet?

I would appreciate your comments when you have an opportunity to respond.

As a positive observation, he really is enjoying learning to spell words, and his most common phrase around home is "How do you spell . . . ?" He seems to know the sounds each letter makes, but sometimes has trouble putting them together. I think he would rather write a word than read it, but it is coming.

At any rate he is content in school and we are pleased with the progress he is making.

I hope you will feel free to contact us if he has any difficulties with any particular area so that we can help him at home in any way we can.

My reply, to which I stapled the three samples of Carl's writing I referred to:

March 8

Thank you for your questions and observations about Carl's writing. I am pleased you decided to ask me about them, as Carl is doing some very important and interesting things right now.

First of all, let's take a look at the three pieces Carl wrote on March 6 during personal writing time. The first piece is a story which he titles "Carl's House." Beneath the title he writes: "There's a sign in my window." If you look at Carl's paper you will notice several important things that tell us what he knows about writing stories.

First of all, he knows that stories usually have a title. He also knows that the title requires its own line and is not part of the story. He knows to begin his story on

the left hand side of the page and go to the right. He uses a combination of capital and small letters, as he is becoming more aware that capitals are used in some places and not in others. He is still not quite sure when to use capitals rather than small letters, but he is moving closer to a traditional format and use. He is also aware that a period is found at the end of a sentence, and although he may not always use one yet, he is aware of their use — another important observation on Carl's part. When writing a story, he stretches it across the page; it is also fairly straight, considering he is still learning to judge the use of space and is concentrating on letter formation.

Do you recall how Carl wrote at the beginning of the year? He wrote and drew with very tiny, restricted movements. He was very self-conscious about it and worried that he couldn't make the letters. He is now much freer in his writing. He writes boldly and requires the large space to master control over forming the letters. They continue to improve, and as I watched him write this piece I recorded that most of his letters were correctly executed — he knew where to begin and end them. Some, like the "o," were made from bottom to top. However he is still mastering this aspect of fine control and it will improve with use.

Now I'd like you to take a look at the second piece Carl wrote. It is a letter and begins "Dear Pam." Right away we can see that Carl knows lots of things about letter writing. He knows that the format is different from that of a story, so he has written what looks like a list. When you think about letters, they are written on smaller pieces of paper, sometimes on notes or cards, so Carl has folded his. There is less space to work with, and the body of the letter is usually found under the salutation. When I asked Carl how he decided to write his letter in this way, he said: "This is the way I write letters. They're not like stories, you know." His letter has a message. He has a sense of audience as he writes a personal message for Pam. I know that Carl is very aware of print at this stage, so I mentioned that usually when you write a letter you put the name of the person next to the "Dear" so it doesn't get mixed up with the message and the person knows right away who it's for.

I left him and moved on to another child, and when I returned Carl had written a third piece: "Dear Kerri." Notice that he has thought over what I said and has incorporated it into his letter. Kerri's name now follows the salutation, and the body of the letter is written below. Again there is a sense of audience and of message. This time he includes his name so there will be no mistaking the sender. Something else is interesting in this piece. We had been talking about the fact that sometimes, as in the word "love," we hear three sounds when there are actually four letters, and I had pointed out that the letter "e" often does that. Look at all the "e's" correctly placed in this piece. Carl is trying out this skill, too, and successfully using it here.

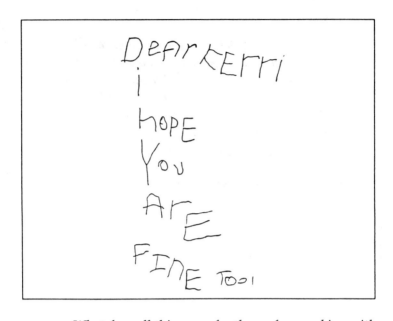

What does all this mean for those of us working with Carl at this important stage in his writing? Well, first of all, we have to be careful not to make him self-conscious about his printing. Yes, some of his letters are a problem right now, but they are steadily improving. A gentle word now and then, with a demonstration of how a letter is formed, is all that is needed. It is important not to overload him at one sitting, so don't demonstrate too many letters at once — one or two in a short piece is all that Carl needs at the moment, since too many will give him a sense of frustration and defeat and we want to avoid that. When I talk to him about letters I don't point out that he may be making the letter incorrectly, but rather that sometimes I find it easier to make an "o" rounder if I "begin it here and go this way." Then I demonstrate on a different piece of paper. This way it doesn't seem like a criticism, and I have offered him an alternative. He may not take me up on it this time, but over time I will see a change. I have to be patient and keep gently trying.

Regarding spaces, Carl already has a sense of individual words as we can see from his letters, with *each word given its own line or space. Right now, in his stories, he is still concentrating on the message and getting it down, and spaces between words have not yet been included. As his writing becomes more relaxed, and as he gets more fluent, the spacing will come. Gently pointing out that spaces help us to read the story will draw Carl's attention to their use. In school we look at spaces and how they are used in the Big Books and charts we read together, as well as in the trade books we have.*

Because he is doing so well in his writing, it's tempting to want to push Carl faster. This could cause more harm than good. Instead, what is needed now is a lot of support, praise and patience. The answers he gets to his letters will inspire him even more to continue writing, and the more he writes the better his writing will get.

I am very pleased you voiced your questions and concerns. I hope this will explain what is going on and how to support it. If you are still concerned or want to talk about this more, then please feel free to phone me and we can make an appointment for you and your husband to come in so we can discuss it more fully. At this point you may not be concerned but just want to know more, and we can talk about children's writing in general and where Carl's writing will go next.

This entry is far more extensive than the others because I felt it was important to address the message between the lines in this parent's entry, and to respond with concrete examples.

The parents enjoyed the dialogue journals even more than I expected. The following are comments made about them during follow-up interviews at the end of the school year:

◆   I think it's a good way to talk to each other. I think when you pick up the children, there are so many parents and children. Even in meetings there are a lot of parents. But with this you can sit down and write down what you really like to and there is nobody to bother you, and Laura brings it home again with some good advice... I really like that she writes back like... try this way or... that's so-and-so in her development. I like that. (Mrs. Sanderson)

♦ That was interesting! I would sit down every couple of days and jot things in it. (Mrs. Dennis)

My responses to some dialogue journal questions and concerns about their child's writing actually helped one family's understanding:

♦ It was sort of a turning point for me because I could finally understand ... you really set it out well and answered all my questions, all my fears kind of vanished when I saw there was progress. (Mrs. Anderson)

And something I hadn't thought of:

♦ Where I am a working parent and can't get into the school as often as I would like ... I enjoyed reading your responses to the little notes I wrote in this book. They helped me to understand Andrew better and let me know what he is like at school and around others. (Mrs. Redden)

One parent shed a little insight into why the journals may not have been used by everyone:

♦ For someone who is used to writing to other people it would be quite easy because they are used to writing down thoughts. For some of us that are used to communicating in person or on the phone, it takes quite a bit of determination to sit down and do it ... Guilt made me decide to write! I decided I hadn't done what I had said I was going to and so I wanted to let you know the things I had noticed and let you know I was still alive! (Mrs. Fisher)

Writing, of course, can reveal a great deal to the writer who may, through writing, achieve a greater understanding of a problem or development, or see an event from a different point of view. Besides, writing helps clarify thoughts and initial impressions. For those parents who tried them, dialogue journals helped them talk to themselves as well as to a supportive listener, allowing them to think on paper about their children and their children's classroom. They also helped me gain greater insight into the parents' thinking and formulate clearer responses to their questions and comments.

Newsletters

Parents want to and need to feel that they know what's going on in their children's classes. For some, the notes I used to send home about upcoming trips or required materials were enough. Others, however, wanted to know more. And in some unfortunate cases parents would miss an event entirely because the note never reached home.

My new spirit inspired me to try a monthly newsletter highlighting past as well as future events (see Appendix D, page 79). I usually describe the theme we are working on and suggest items the children might bring from home to make the whole experience more enjoyable. I draw attention to some of our special events, dates important to the families as well as the school — in-service days, holidays, meetings, children's birthdays. The newsletter also briefly enumerates the visitors we've had: who they were, why they came, what they did and talked about. In any that follow a class meeting I put a summary of the meeting so those who weren't able to attend can keep up with what's going on and won't feel excluded from our family circle.

To make writing the newsletters easier I use a notebook to jot down, as they occur, any events I feel newsworthy, so I won't have to struggle to remember the things we've done over the past month as I scramble madly to meet a deadline — usually the first Monday of the month. I read the whole newsletter to the children before it goes out so they know what's in it. I find they are more likely to deliver it if they are in a position to supplement the news it contains, and the parents more likely to read it if the children point out the highlights.

I limit the newsletter to a single page, emphasizing items with eye-catching graphics. Computer software programs such as Print Shop, Print Master and The Newsroom make the publication attractive and easy to do. With the first issue I send home a magnet with a suggestion that the newsletter be posted on the refrigerator for easy reference.

Parents are always loud in their appreciation of the newsletter, often making a point of coming to school after the first one goes out in October to say they hope it will continue throughout the year. By the last one in June most are thoroughly hooked and express the hope that next year's teacher will produce a similar newsletter.

♦   It was a good communication because . . . there were some things you might have missed unless you grilled your child at the end of the day — and that you don't want to do! They usually mentioned the themes, which gave you the chance to ask if they were going to take something in for it and to keep your eye out for things that relate to it. (Mrs. Fisher)

♦   I really like it. I think every teacher should have that! You know what's going on all the time. (Mrs. Beck)

An unexpected benefit was suggested by Marie's mom:

♦   I've kept all those and put them in her little treasure book . . . when the year is done, and she's older, I can sit and say . . . "These are the things you did when you were little. These were your main events in life in your first year in school." I think it's the best memory she could have of her first year. (Mrs. Carr)

Teachers often assume that parents know, by telepathy, what's coming up on the school calendar and what's going on in the classroom. If parents are confused or apparently uninterested, teachers have a tendency to blame either the family for not reading the notices or the child for not delivering them. Newsletters become a special means of communication that both parents and children look forward to. When they are produced on a regular basis, their arrival is keenly anticipated, and if a single copy goes astray it becomes the object of an earnest search. Parents need to be kept informed, and in my experience they value the extra effort it takes on the part of the teacher for them to be so.

Book bags

Weekly children's bags

It's one thing to explain to parents the benefits of reading aloud to their children, but quite another to provide them with the means of making it a favorite habit. Several things work against this. For instance, in my area some people have to travel a great distance to reach a bookstore — and once they are there, many of them feel uncertain about what to buy, especially since books are so costly. Our small-town public library system, while excellent, has a good but relatively small collection that spreads over several branches, as well as a bookmobile that serves the rural areas. Even so, few parents request specific books.

It became clear to me that most parents are probably unfamiliar with the wealth of good children's literature now available, and that I needed to help them by getting good books into their homes on a regular basis. I therefore developed a set of book bags, enough for every child to take a different one home every week — a project I was able to fund, in part, with a startup grant from my provincial teachers' union.

Each bag was organized around a different theme or author: the Robert Munsch bag, the Dr. Seuss bag, the Clifford bag, the bear bag, the space bag, the dinosaur bag and so on, and each contained four or five books. I tried to include some hardcover books I thought the parents might find expensive, along with the more accessible paperbacks — both good quality read-aloud stories and predictable books the children might be familiar with from school. These I hoped, after repeated readings, the children would begin to read on their own. In some of the bags I included a book with an accompanying tape, since I knew the taped story would provide a good oral reading model for both parents and children. I also made available, on loan, an inexpensive tape recorder with rechargeable batteries. Appendix E (page 80) provides the text of a booklet I included. Its purpose was to underline the importance of reading to children, to explain how the book bag project works, and to provide hints for parents not only for keeping track of the materials in the bag but also, more important, for setting aside time to read with their children on a regular basis.

I also decided to include other materials related to the books or the theme, to encourage ways of responding to the literature through music, movement, puppetry and art: a bear puppet, plastic dinosaur figures, a calendar with movable vinyl weather and special-event stickers, etc.

To make it easier for the parents to round up the contents, I put everything in an attractive children's tote bag, along with an index card listing the contents of the bag. A local travel agent donated tags and I marked them

36

with the name of the program (It's All in the Bag) and my name and room number. On the other side I put the name of the bag and a designated number (Fairy Tales #4).

One week before sending the bags out for the first time I sent a letter home that explained the program to the parents, asking them to watch for the bags on a specified date. I tried to make it clear that I realized some things would get lost and others would wear out, and that in either case all I needed was a note sent back with the bag so I could replace the item. This was important because I didn't want worried parents to restrict their children's use of the bag.

The book bags went out each Wednesday evening and were returned the following Wednesday morning, with the stipulation that the next bag wouldn't be sent until the previous one was returned. By following a Wednesday to Wednesday instead of Monday to Friday routine I ensured that the bags were in the homes over the weekend. Working parents, I thought, might not get to them before then.

The project worked better than I could ever have imagined. As each child returned a bag on Wednesday morning I immediately assigned a new number, but didn't give out the bags until just before the end of the day. By then my room was filled with excitement and anticipation as the children wondered what treasures their new bags would hold. They gathered on the floor to wait for their names to be called and their bags handed out, all the while making comments about the bags they'd already had: "That's got a great book in it." "That's the bag with the skipping rope!" "I like the tape in that bag."

The children then found a place at a table or on the floor to explore the contents of their bags. Some found familiar stories and began reading them; others were intrigued by new titles and couldn't wait to get home for someone to read to them. Even those who forgot to return their bags got a new one (I had made up five extra ones), although they couldn't take it home that day. Instead they took home a reminder — and the new bags almost always went home the next day.

The feedback I received from parents was equally exciting. The bags had benefits I hadn't even considered! The parents enjoyed the steady supply of different books, and many made the arrival of the bags on Wednesday a special event eagerly looked forward to.

- Wednesdays are a big deal here. We can hardly wait until Wednesday after supper. (Mrs. Lamb)

In some cases the demand by the child was so great that:

- As soon as they're in the door she has to have them read and then Robert [younger preschooler] has to have them read. (Mrs. Carr)

The kinds of books in the bags also made an impression on the parents:

- Stores . . . don't carry books that I'm interested in seeing my kids have . . . This way it's all picked out to her age and what she's reading and what she's hearing. To me it's something she can relate to . . . rather than something too old or too young. (Mrs. Evens)

- Now I've bought Tess some different ones. Like I bought her the Wacky Word Book and I would never have bought that. I've seen it on the shelf and thought, oh, that's just a bunch of gobbledy goop, but they got such a big kick out of it . . . It shows me what they're interested in. (Mrs. Long)

- We have a cassette player and she is able to play them. I have concentrated now on picking up more of those tapes . . . I hadn't noticed it before and I could have kicked myself . . . but when she had one of those book bags home the other week and was reading the stories while the tape was playing . . . I thought if I go to those bookstores and pick out some of those books and tapes, that way there will be stories that she'll be interested in . . . and not be stuck on . . . and later on when there is nobody available to read to her she can take a tape and put it in the machine and take the book and go along with it. She'll associate what they're saying with what's actually in the book. (Mrs. Fisher)

The book bags made the sharing of favorite stories a habit in most homes. A ritual was established around them, from choosing which books to read first to the rules regarding their handling. It was clear that the program was enjoyed by both parents and children and would be missed when the children moved on to the next class, unless that class had a similar program.

◆ Next year we will have to go more to the library and get more books . . . we are not going to have the book bag any more! (Mrs. Beck)

By bringing quality books into the home on a regular basis I was able to provide the parents with a steady supply of reading materials, as well as a wide sampling of the kinds of books they might purchase from the bookstore or borrow from the library. They viewed the book bags as a service appreciated by the whole family. The bags became part of their home routines and had a lasting effect on their children's reading habits.

Monthly parent bags

Parents face many pressures today. In our fast-paced world, parents — working and single parents in particular — sometimes find themselves faced with a shortage of time and energy to devote to their children. They often wonder how to manage their day-to-day activities and still provide their children with enough loving attention and interesting things to do. For some, the burden of household management seems almost overwhelming, but they find it difficult to admit they need help. Their problems bring tension and unrest to normal family affairs. They feel guilty and alone.

As a parent of two children myself, and working outside the home, I've found books a valuable source of information about many aspects of child-raising. I remember scrounging bookstores for books about birthday parties, discipline and a host of other topics as they became important in our lives. That's not to say those books had all the answers. But I found it comforting to know I wasn't the only one to have encountered a particular problem. So it occurred to me that a natural extension of the children's home book bag project would be a similar one for parents.

This time I made duplicate sets of bags with 15 books in each set. The luggage tag attached to each bag noted the title of the project (Tot Totes), an identifying bag number and my name and room number. Scheduling was a simple matter, with bags going out on the first Monday of the month and coming back to me on the last. That allowed me time to check the bag contents and read any comments the parents might have made.

I included titles I felt parents would be interested in reading, some of a practical nature full of parenting tips and make-and-do activities, others explaining the reading and writing process from a whole language perspective. Appendix F (page 83) lists and describes many of those titles.

Along with each book I included a letter, in a colorful duotang folder so it wouldn't be misplaced, in which I tried to describe the book and what led me to select it. Appendix G (page 90) shows the type of letter I wrote.

In the back of each book I taped an index card with the heading "What did you think?" After reading the book myself I made a brief comment on the card about some part that I found helpful or that I especially enjoyed, and invited the parents to do the same. The remarks that came back revealed how different books appealed to different people. They indicated the enjoyment the parents got from some books and the usefulness of the information they found in others, and in general reflected their writers' involvement and enthusiasm for this project. These are some of the comments:

♦ Enjoyed the book. It made me realize the full return of reading aloud. It explained the how, when, and also the care in selecting the right type of books according to the child. By the way — I would rather read a good book myself than watch the box!

♦ A nice way to find out what your child would do in this situation.

♦ Light but humorous messages — I liked the section about failing English: pp. 32, 131!

♦ Your Own Grades — pp. 83-85 — reminds me of my own school years and it is going to happen again with our children!

♦ Nice to be able to laugh at child raising, even though the same kinds of things happen to ourselves. Liked the reasoning of pp. 57-59.

♦ So many games, in and out of doors!

♦ Very helpful with problems such as allowances, especially Chapter 4.

These comments, and many more like them, demonstrate that the parents were reading the books, enjoying them and making use of the ideas. For one parent in particular, The Craft of Children's Writing (1984) by Judith Newman caused a breakthrough in understanding. She commented:

◆ This book explained it [the development of writing] really well. It showed a child writing random letters and the person writing the book said "And this means . . . and a couple of months later when they are writing . . . it means . . ." I even went and told a friend of mine about it. He was really upset and worried that his kid was never going to write . . . And I said "This is great. Don't worry about it, it's going to be all right!" (Mrs. Hart)

The parents were extremely pleased. Some phoned to find out where I had purchased a particular book because they wanted their own copy. Bill Cosby's Fatherhood was so popular that it made the entire rounds of friends and relatives during the time it was with one family. I enjoyed selecting the books and continue to add titles as I discover them — often from the parents themselves, who have begun recommending books for me to include.

Teachers assume that parents know about parenting, that they're confident about what they're doing. But most parents worry they might not be doing the right thing for their children. They wonder if the stages the children are going through are normal — and whether they'll survive them. Book bags for parents offer much more than just a ready-made library coming into the home; they provide parents with another kind of support, one that says "I don't know all the answers either, but I can help you find some possible solutions."

Parent/teacher meetings

In my experience, good attendance at parent/teacher nights is the exception rather than the rule, for several reasons. Frequently parents have prior commitments. For some, babysitters are a problem. Those who have more than one child in school have a problem attending meetings held in different classrooms at the same time, and usually end up visiting the teacher of the child with the most problems.

When I set out to improve my relationship with parents I established as my goal at least a fifty percent attendance rate at every meeting. First I needed a drawing card they couldn't resist — their own children! About a month before the first meeting I took slides of the children engaging in the kind of reading and writing activities they would be involved in during a normal day, making sure to include each element of my program described in the parent booklet (Appendix B, page 73). I also made sure that every child was in at least one photograph. I took particular pains to make clear what it was the children were doing and, with the help of a friend, included shots of myself in action.

The children were wonderful! I had carefully explained that I would be showing the slides to their parents to explain the kinds of things they were doing in my classroom and that I wanted them to do just what they normally did. I also mentioned that we would arrange a special night for their parents to see the slides. The children thought that was great and happily demonstrated what they do in the course of a school day.

When the developed slides came back I prepared a slide-talk for the parents showing their children as learners. I included a notice of the upcoming event in the newsletter and scheduled the meeting for a night without other school activities. I sent the invitations home with the children a week ahead of time — making sure, of course, that the children knew what was in them! I mentioned that any parents without a sitter should feel free to bring their children along, and I raved about the slides and the great job the children had done. (I also mentioned how I would be using the slides in future workshops and presentations.) And they came. Nineteen of 24 families were represented, in most cases by both parents and in some by the whole family. I was absolutely amazed and thrilled! I had a feeling that this meeting was the most important step of all in getting me and my parents on common ground when talking about what school was like for their children. Here is what the parents had to say later:

- It's hard to see them go off to school. By seeing the slides I could see what Marie was doing in my mind any time of the day. I would just close my eyes and see her in the book area or playing with the puppets . . . (Mrs. Carr)

- What I found . . . sometimes when you take pictures of children they want to be stars of the show, but they were good that way — they were just themselves, so, for whomever the slides were meant for, for teaching purposes, they would be able to get more out of them and even parents could see them acting in a realistic manner . . . and how smoothly things do run in a normal day. (Mrs. Fisher)

Throughout the year I had other meetings, although none with the same tremendous turnout. However, by that time I was more comfortable with the idea that reaching and supporting even one parent was worth the effort. I had workshops on a variety of topics. At the writing workshop, for instance, I talked about writing in the home, how absolutely natural it is and why it's so important. I spoke of my own family and my friends and neighbors, describing the kinds of literacy events we all shared. I used actual samples and we talked about them together. The parents were very enthusiastic, and some shared their own family experiences:

- I have heard a lot about reading to children so they can have a better chance at learning to read, but I never thought about writing in the same way. (Mr. Dill)

- I guess we don't write very much with our children . . . now, wait a minute, of course we do! You just showed us that! I guess I never put much value on grocery lists or letters to grandma before. (Mrs. Alport)

I also held a night where parents could come in and use the computers and programs their children were using. My husband, Steve, volunteered to answer questions about purchasing personal computers.

The key to all this lies in tapping the interests of the parents. If there is something they are interested in, or want to know more about, they come willingly. Here are some of their notes:

- Sorry we couldn't make it to the slide-show. Do you think you could run it on an afternoon after school? (Mrs. Collins)
- We can't come to the computer meeting tonight — Beaver banquet — but we're still interested. (Mrs. Phillips)

Or by phone:

- We were all set to come tonight but Chris came down with the flu. Next time I'm at school when you're in the computer room, maybe I could stop in and have a look. (Mr. Hart)

It's high time that meetings took on a new look. In a fast-paced, busy society, school meetings have to compete with recreational pursuits, personal advancement courses and social events. Parents need to feel the meetings they are asked to attend are tailored to their needs, that the school is offering them something they want. They need to feel they have a personal interest in what is being offered and that careful thought has gone into the planning. When meetings are planned in this way parents want to be there and will make every effort to do so.

Summary

These are the projects I initiated over time. I wondered, as I started each one, if it would make any difference at all in the way I was communicating with parents or they with me. It almost always takes a while for a new project to become established, for even the smallest sign that someone out there is making use of your efforts.

But I tried not to feel discouraged or frustrated if parents didn't write in their journals, attend meetings or comment on the cards in the books. I looked at the projects as a normal part of my job. I didn't feel I needed special recognition or a pat on the back for doing them; I simply enjoyed them and had faith that they would make a difference in the long run. Nor did I expect that the projects I was doing then would be the only ones I'd ever try. I knew I'd continue to add to and modify them as my relationship with parents changed and grew.

Sharing observations

Yetta Goodman has written a lot about the need for teachers to be "kid-watchers." Parents have been kid-watching for at least five years before their children enter school, and this makes them invaluable assistants in gathering data about their children's literacy development, not only within the school context but in other contexts as well.

I overheard the following conversation between two parents at the local swimming pool:

Parent A: (referring to a young child about one year old) "Is she talking very much yet?"

Parent B: "Oh, yes, she's been saying lots of words for quite a while now. But just last week she started putting things together into sentences — not very long ones, mind you, but they are coming."

Most parents are good observers of their children's growth at home. They notice improvement in a sport or hobby, a physical growth spurt, or the use of more complex sentence structures in oral language. They make these observations based on certain expectations or perceptions they've developed through experience. If they are new parents, they may welcome advice and comments from other family members or friends. In most cases their observations are influenced by the community and culture in which the family lives, and interpreted in the light of their own or others' prior experiences.

The parents of the children in my class seemed to develop a new understanding and acceptance of the literacy behavior they were observing in their children as a result of our joint efforts at reciprocal communication. Before, some may not have recognized such behavior, or may have dismissed it as insignificant or meaningless. But the wide variety of projects we undertook helped them to interpret literacy behavior for what it really was, and to put it into a meaningful framework which they felt included them, as evidenced in the dialogue journals, and which now made perfect sense to them. Their observations gave evidence of deep reflection and self-analysis as their understanding gradually developed. And in my journal responses I either confirmed their predictions or encouraged them to rethink from another perspective.

At the end of the school year I interviewed the parents (see Appendix H, page 91) to assess their reactions to the year's work. They commented not only on the various projects but also on their children's literacy development, and they couldn't help but share literacy stories when they spoke about their children's growth over the year.

Together the dialogue journals and these interviews provided me with additional insight into the changes I felt I had observed in the parents. My main impression was that, on the whole, they seemed more articulate, open and willing to share their observations. Now it seemed that we shared the same mental image of how literacy learning develops and how it can best be supported. As they related incidents from their daytime or bedtime story reading sessions, they were beginning to use the same kind of language whole language teachers use in retelling their literacy stories.

If you remember, in the parent survey I conducted before the children started school 19 of 24 parents expressed uncertainty about their children's reading preferences — that is, they were unable to name a favorite story — and 17 of 19 voiced annoyance at being asked to read a story more than once in a sitting. But that had changed. Now the parents talked more about particular books and favorite kinds of stories. And they related incidents that showed how repeated readings and discussions about favorite stories were becoming a common practice:

◆ I find that Carl loves to be read stories. It seems to take me hours to get finished one book. But I like that 'cos [sic] it proves to me that he is absorbing all that I read to him. (Mrs. Alport)

◆ Laura really wanted to have this particular book. It was a cat and they took a pan and forgot to put holes for the ears in it . . . she just loved that book . . . even the name made her start laughing. She wanted to hear the book again. We didn't feel like hearing it again, but in the end Meg was having a good time and Laura was having a good time and I was having a good time! So it was good to do that book for a second and third time! (Mrs. Barr)

◆ Dr. Seuss, Tess loves Dr. Seuss. And we read them over and over. I think she likes the rhyming. (Mrs. Long)

◆ Steven has said he enjoys the listening center at school. He said that way he gets to hear the stories he likes over and over. I asked if he wanted me to read stories at home over and over. He said "Oh, yes. But if you don't want to maybe you can make me a tape." I didn't realize he would be interested in hearing them so much. (Mrs. Paris)

The parents were also noticing strategies their children were employing while reading. For example, reconstruction of meaning, sometimes seemingly from memory, is often of concern to parents, but now this stage of literacy development was beginning to be valued as an appropriate activity:

- Charles will ask for one story repeatedly (I read *Old Yeller* four times one afternoon) then he reads it to me. He now seems more interested in some books for the story than for the pictures. (Mrs. Thomas)

- When Marie and I sit down to read her books we read a lot of short story books mainly because she can repeat and memorize them. After which she sits and reads to her brother. She is starting to recognize words using the method of using our fingers to run along phrases when we read. She never tires of any of the books. (Mrs. Dennis)

- If I'm a little slow getting up, he will sit on his bed and "picture read" some books in his room. He tends to do this often. If you listen carefully as he "reads" (as long as he doesn't know you're doing so) he'll follow his finger along the words and sometimes say some of the things from the picture. When asked to tell what he's doing, he'll say: "Reading, Mom." (Mrs. Wick)

- With a book like Dr. Seuss, we start out reading together, but halfway through Laura likes to read to me, not from the pictures. She remembers the words that are coming back all the time. Those are good books to learn from! (Mrs. Barr)

- I think memory is a form of reading, too, because if you don't know what the story is about or what the whole concept is, it's pretty hard to understand what you are saying — then it becomes just a bunch of words not a story. (Mrs. Saunders)

Although parents still described this activity as "memory reading" (a misnomer and, in my opinion, a relic of previous school contacts), their comments demonstrated a growing acceptance of what the children were doing and a recognition of the reconstruction of text as an important literacy development.

Even other family members were beginning to develop a greater sense of value for observed literacy behavior. Often discussions that helped older siblings understand what the younger ones were doing happened during family shared reading times:

- When Laura reads a word that's not exactly there, Meg starts to tell her and Laura gets upset sometimes. So I tell Meg just to stop helping her because Laura isn't ready for it yet and she can tell it in her own words . . . and we just have to temper her a little. (Mrs. Barr)

- The girls are supportive of Carol's reading because they themselves have had reading disabilities or problems. I think they actually recognize, inside them anyway, that Carol needs to learn and they know it's not easy . . . they know reading is important, to learn . . . (Mrs. Fisher)

The quality of the observations being made by older siblings was reflected in this one written in a dialogue journal by Christopher's fourteen-year-old sister:

- Today while we were reading Where the Wild Things Are Christopher said: "The pictures always go with the words." (Christine Hart)

Parents also seemed aware of literacy milestones and valued them in the same way they had valued their children's first steps and first words. They were willing and eager to share these with me, as well as with neighbors and friends:

◆ Christopher's most extensive writing so far:

Picture drawn of PAPE (puppy) with speech balloon

Exciting!" (Mr. Hart)

◆ Laura was looking in a book and told me "Mom, this is the O for love and the E and in this word there is an L and a V. If you put these words together and take the other letters out then you have LOVE!!" (Mrs. Barr)

◆ She came home from school with a book . . . it was one of the Meg and Mog books and the word "pandemonium" was in it. She brought this book in and she says "Mommy, Mommy, come here quickly." I rushed in the room . . . and she read the whole book through and when she got to the part with this big word she read "And pandemonium broke out." . . . I said how did you know that word and she said, "Well, Mrs. Baskwill read this to me the other day. Today I read this one myself." That's the first time she ever said that! (Mrs. Long)

Now the parents' support for their children's literacy development seemed to be present in much the same way as it had been for oral language development throughout the preschool years. They supported approximations and participated uncritically in the literacy activities initiated by their children:

◆ After suppertime Laura started to talk about the books she made at school. She counted four books and she gave us (daddy, sister and me) a "diarrea" book. Laura was so happy to share that we didn't explain to her that anything was wrong with her "diarrea" books. (Mrs. Barr)

- I think Roger has more hand coordination with a pencil and he can draw a reasonable picture of a house and a stick person . . . even a fish isn't too bad. As long as he's satisfied. Now a lot of the pictures he brings home from school don't look like anything to me, but I'll ask him what it is and he will say what it is to him. And I'll say "Fine, that's great!" (Mrs. Wick)

- I've got a letter Marie wrote to Tom and me and we want to keep that one. It's really cute. If you really look at the words you can see what she's written but you almost have to kind of play around a little bit to see what she's written. It says: "Dear Mommy and Daddy, I'm writing this letter to tell you that I love you." . . . we've given it to people to read and they're going "Oh, isn't that nice." They can pick out certain words and that's it. But we can sit there and read it. We understand what she's saying! (Mrs. Carr)

Finally, the parents expressed their support and growing understanding of whole language teaching and the classroom program. The Andersons' change in understanding came about as a result of their child's growth in writing and their own observations of that growth:

- Our expectations are much more positive, much more accepting; a better approach to his responses. Now I see that it's the content and what they think it is and the whole language concept. (Mrs. Anderson)

- I wasn't sure what the concept was either. The more we found out and the more we learned and that letter that Anne wrote and the one Mrs. Baskwill wrote back . . . everything is coming together. I've been on a course for work and what they're teaching us there and what's going on at school is starting to make lots of sense. Give the children a lot more time and a lot more responsibility and not saying you have to sit in a desk. It's your own responsibility to learn. When I was in school they had to pull it out of us. I'm sort of jealous that I didn't have this when I went to school. I can see that learning this way would be a lot more fun. (Mr. Anderson)

♦ You know, in the past children were not always able to meet the "standards" imposed on them by teachers and schools. Some children had problems yet they weren't "stupid," they just couldn't meet those standards. Some children may not be able to learn what others can or as fast. They need time. The most important thing is that they not feel down about it or themselves. As I often tell my kids, "You're human, you're not perfect. You just have to work as hard as you can." Now, in this whole language, teachers are saying what I have always known in my heart. (Mrs. Fisher)

These anecdotes from parents, and many more like them, helped confirm my belief that my relationship with those parents was different from the ones I'd had in the past with other parents. We were operating like a family, keeping in touch regularly in a variety of ways, sharing a common interest in the well-being of the children and developing a sense of mutual respect and understanding.

Even more remarkable was that these parents were no different, in the beginning, from the many parents whose children I had taught in other years. What was different was our relationship at the end of the year.

Making it work

The projects I've described here take a lot of work; whole language teaching is always a lot of work. However, you can ease your way into a satisfying and rewarding dialogue and relationship with parents. Not everything needs to begin at the same time, or even in the same year. After you try one project and get it well established, you'll feel more confident about trying another. Once you get into the habit of writing daily notes, answering dialogue journals and preparing newsletters, you'll find yourself doing them in spare moments during the day, filling spaces of time that might otherwise be spent waiting for a doctor's appointment, the end of your child's ballet lesson, or the beginning of a staff meeting. You'll find that what might once have seemed totally overwhelming will eventually fall into your schedule without demanding too much of your time.

Nevertheless, it pays to attend to details to make a project run as efficiently as possible. If you find checking book bags taking an inordinate amount of time during or after school, try having grade six students check them for you. If your typing is laborious, or you end up putting off your newsletter so long that you spend the night before putting it out, ask a parent, a colleague, or perhaps your spouse to take over the typing for you. If you do, however, be sure to prepare the copy well in advance to allow the typist ample time to get back to you with questions and problems.

It also helps to spread the start times for your projects out over the year. Besides being more manageable for you, phasing projects in may prove less overwhelming for parents. It will help to establish a timeline at the beginning of the year for the start of each project. Even though you may not be able to adhere to it precisely, it will allow you to do some rough forward planning. This, for example, is the one I use:

June 23	Meeting and booklet for incoming parents, children's play day
Sept. 5	First notes home
Sept. 15	Children's book bags
Oct. 1	First newsletter
Nov. 1	Parents' book bags
Nov. 5	Slide show, dialogue journals
Mar. 8	Writing workshop
May 10	Computer workshop

You might add school-wide parent/teacher nights and report card conferences to this timeline to give you an overall picture of the year. I display copies of mine prominently, both at school and at home, so I can keep on top of my deadlines. Sometimes things get a little hectic, especially when report cards are due or there's illness at home, but with a little adjustment I'm usually back on track before long.

For me, this "new" approach to parent/teacher communication is no longer new — it's now eight years since I first became aware of the need. Looking back, I realize that each year I've learned something new from the parents — yet I know how much there is left to learn. It hasn't all been smooth sailing, of course. I've had to work very hard to establish communication with some parents, and I'm sure some have felt it was hard for them to communicate with me. But over time we've all become better at it, and there's no doubt in my mind that we've developed a sense of shared responsibility for "our" children's learning. Here is yet another parent comment, from a casual conversation in a cornfield two years ago when I stopped to buy corn:

♦ You know, I was thinking about what you told us about reading. I used to think that Cindy talked too much when I read to her. She always has something to say about the story or the pictures or she wants to read with me. I used to try to keep her quiet, but that wasn't easy to do. Then I saw on the video how you wanted the children to read along and how they talked about the story or asked questions. Now I see that Cindy will fit right in. She can do that well and will not be bad like I thought she would be if she talked like that. Now it's more fun to read, now that I don't have to keep her quiet. You know, she's a pretty smart kid! (Mrs. Peal)

I know that some teachers are uncomfortable with the idea of becoming familiar with parents. Is a child's home life any of our business? I used to think not myself. But what happens to an individual affects that individual whether it happens at home, at school, at work or at play. Within the family model it's natural for the teacher to become part of the lives of the children's families.

Parents come to accept this mutual support system. At the pool I hear what a particular child is reading now, or I'm asked about a child's stage of writing development. At the ball field I'm questioned about a child's attentiveness, or asked about the best way to handle temper tantrums. Parents are looking for places to air problems and share triumphs — and so, for that matter, are teachers. And both groups want to share their problems and triumphs with someone they trust.

Besides, it's exciting to hear about the children I've been so close to for the past 10 months. Too often I used to lose track of their growth as they moved on to the next grade. Now I get the news along with the rest of the family! For instance, about six days into one school year I received a phone call from the very upset parent of a child I had taught the preceding year:

◆ I just put Jennie on the bus. I mean I actually put her on the bus — me in my pajamas! She was crying and didn't want to go, but I heard your voice in my head telling me I had to get her there, and that she would be all right once she got to school. I didn't know who else to turn to but I knew I could call you. Could you check on her when she gets to school and see how she's making out? (Mrs. Aimes)

Of course I could! After all, isn't that what families are for?

My thoughts about my relationship with the parents of my students have changed so much over the last few years that I often forget how different that relationship is from the one many teachers have. It was brought home to me in the school office late last year as I was showing off photos of my class that I'd taken on the first day of school.

Another teacher: "Oh, photos?"

Me: "Yes, of my kids."

(She took a quick look through the photographs.)

Teacher: "These are your school kids. I thought they were of your own kids — of your family."

Me: "They are of my family — it's just gotten a bit bigger lately!"

A word of caution: we must remember that it's not our job to try to change or pass judgment on family life styles. It is our job, however, to give and receive advice, make suggestions and act as a sounding board to help parents think through a problem and develop their own solutions.

Just as we recognize differences in the children and expect growth to take place over time, so we must with their parents. It takes time for a new picture to develop. It takes time for a relationship to become established, especially one that offers real insights and observations, and above all, since a support group must operate on trust rather than blame, one in which each partner is willing to withhold judgment of the other.

Once this happens, whole language teachers and parents will truly become partners in the process, sharing both the responsibility and the joy of nurturing the development of their childrens' literacy learning.

Moving on

Learning is never finished. After completing the first part of this book I moved to another school where, as principal, I was determined to establish the kind of two-way communication between parents and staff that I'd come to expect. I wondered if the projects I'd already tried would be appropriate for this new community, and how they'd be received by these parents. I was now in a different position — instead of developing projects over time I could set them up ready-made, although with people who didn't know me.

There were a few wrinkles I hadn't anticipated. At first parents thought the dialogue journals meant their children were having trouble in school. When I investigated the reason, I discovered that a teacher from another school had offered that explanation. So I learned an important lesson: even if I think I've explained something well on paper, I can't take for granted that parents will understand. Dialogue journals require face-to-face explanation, something I'd forgotten in the busy start of a new year. As a result, it took longer than I'd anticipated to get adequate participation. I'll avoid that problem from now on by meeting in the spring with the parents of the five-year-olds about to enter school.

Basically, however, I find these parents much the same as those I left behind. They want to become involved in their children's learning and ensure their success, but they don't understand the changes taking place in education and appreciate whatever help the school is willing to offer. They have a wealth of information about their children to share, but until now they've never been approached to share it. Although from very different communities, the two sets of parents have much in common when it comes to their children. And it's my feeling that this would be true of most parents, regardless of their geographic area.

So I've continued to develop projects, some specifically for the parents of the children in my own class (I still teach a primary group) and some for the entire school. I've also discovered others, like myself, who see a need to communicate more effectively with parents, and I've been in touch with teachers, school boards and universities who are initiating similar projects.

In this section I'd like to share some of my new projects. Like the earlier ones, these are based on the family model, but since I'm now thinking of the whole school rather than just my own class, some of them are more general in nature. My staff shares my thinking and many projects now involve parents across grades, most of them very effectively. The teachers are impressed by how much their communication with parents has improved, how much more readily parents accept and understand any changes they implement, and how much greater the parents' desire to be involved in their children's education has become.

Lunch box launchers

This past year two main curriculum areas were targeted for in-service by our school district: math and science. Within those areas the focus was on such things as philosophy, objectives, ways to improve methodology, materials and evaluation. Meanwhile my new school had decided that one of its goals for the year would be to work at improving communication with parents.

In an effort to combine the school's goal with that of the district, I developed a project that would allow parents to participate in math, science and social studies activities. I hoped the activities would help parents better understand the concepts being dealt with in these curriculum areas and make them feel that this kind of knowledge was no longer beyond their experience.

The idea was to develop, for each grade level, approximately 10 boxes of take-home materials that would fit inside the children's lunch boxes or totes. Each contained a book that became the "launcher" for the activity (see Appendix I, page 96), plus whatever materials were needed to carry the activity out. There were also two cards, one describing the concept or skill that was being practiced and another listing the contents of the box, so the parents would know exactly what it should include when it arrived home.

I had to do quite a lot of searching for just the right books to include as launchers. Sometimes appropriate books weren't available and I substituted an activity card describing what the parents could do with the materials.

The boxes were usually signed out for a single evening or weekend (each had a luggage tag with the name and number of the box to make it easy to keep track of), but they were also used during the day, either as learning center activities or as free choice materials. The resource teacher also had access to them, as did cross-age tutors and parent volunteers.

It's too soon to know what impact this project may have on parents' understanding of the ways science, math and social studies are being taught. However, I do know parents are enjoying it:

- ◆ I didn't like helping Roy with his homework, but I really look forward to those lunch boxes. (Mrs. Evens)

- ◆ I'm amazed at what Cindy is able to do with those pattern blocks! She had me try some and it took me a while to finally figure out the pattern. (Mrs. Wilson)

- ◆ I hated science when I was in school. Dan comes running in the door with this "science box" and wants me to stop whatever I'm doing to help him with his experiment. Now the whole family gets into the act. When my husband's home he wants to try it too! (Mrs. Deal)

School effectiveness and student achievement are strongly influenced by parents' involvement in their children's learning. I hope that, through projects like this one, parents will feel that working with their children in math, science and social studies is well within their capability and control.

Activity calendars

Calendars play an important role in my home, helping the family keep track of deadlines, important events and milestones of growth. Together we record new information as we get it and adjust our schedules as we need to.

I decided that a parent/child activity calendar might provide a way of communicating with parents about some of the activities my own family has had fun with while at the same time showing them how to help their children develop an understanding of the passage of time. I was able to obtain a grant from our teachers' union to cover the cost of an illustrator and the printing.

The calendar spanned thirteen months, September to September, so it could be distributed to the children on the first day of school and continue through the following summer. Each month was planned around a theme and contained a poem, a short bibliography of five children's books, a science activity, a reading/writing activity, a recipe and a craft (see Appendix J, page 94).

Both children and parents had a wonderful time with the calendar activities. The children often told me about the ones they tried, or brought in the crafts they made, or gave us samples of their cooking. Parents sent in suggestions for future calendars.

♦ Cathy, Meg and I have enjoyed the calendar. Our favorite was the balloon rocket. We had a lot of fun making that one go . . . I am sending you a copy of a science activity I cut out from a magazine. Maybe you can make use of it in a future issue . . . By the way, it really works! (Mrs. Watson)

♦ We found the calendar a great place to keep track of special things which happened during the year — like a diary. I'm going to save it for Kim when the year is over. Some day she'll want to look back over her early school days and she'll have this as a memento. (Mrs. Anders)

A side benefit of the calendar is that it helps parents establish important organizational habits with their children, as they record when special materials are needed, when important events are taking place, and when there'll be no school!

♦ We got in the habit of checking the calendar at night before bed to see if Ricky needed to bring anything special. The other night . . . we were amazed to see he had a half-day the next day. We had forgotten all about it . . . Thank goodness for the calendar! (Mrs. Allen)

Some parents found they hadn't thought to do certain activities with their children until they saw them suggested in the calendar. Others remembered doing similar activities when they were children themselves.

♦ I had forgotten how much fun bubble blowing could be! We used to mix up our own bubble solution when we were kids. Thanks for the recipe! (Mrs. Wilcox)

A parent/child activity calendar needn't be as elaborate as the one I put together. You can also prepare a monthly version on the photocopier or Gestetner using your own illustrations. The purpose is simply to model the kinds of quality-time experiences parents and children can have together, and to provide busy parents with ready-made ideas from which to choose. A calendar doesn't put any pressure on parents; it's just there if and when they decide to take advantage of it.

Pamphlets and booklets

I've found that parents appreciate having specific information on various aspects of the school program. They can take pamphlets and booklets home, read them any number of times, in private, and think about their contents before coming to school for a talk or phoning with additional questions.

One of the first booklets I distributed was a student organizer for children in grades three to six. Although it was designed for children to use, it also included a letter to parents describing the importance of an organizer and suggesting ways to improve or develop good study habits. My husband Steve, who had developed an organizer for his school, was generous enough to allow me to adopt his format for mine.

The organizer covered one-third of the school year. It contained a calendar page and daily diary pages for recording specific assignments. Its limited time span wasn't forbidding to either parents or children and its colorful cover made it readily recognizable.

An organizer picks up where an activity calendar leaves off. It continues to encourage parents to know what projects or special events their children have and keeps them up to date on daily assignments. Parents seemed to appreciate the organizer and quickly saw its benefits:

- Dan has done really well this year. I think it was because of those organizers. I finally knew what he was supposed to do and he knew I knew so he didn't try to get out of doing it! (Mrs. Deal)

- Ellen thought the organizer was a great idea. She has always been such a worrier. Now she knows all she has to do is write it down and she'll get it in on time. Now she just worries about losing the organizer! (Mrs. Dickens)

- My husband thought it was your [the school's] job to look after whether Mary did her homework. When you told us about how the organizer worked, he thought it wouldn't make a difference. But we decided to try it and see. We even did some of the things it suggested, like set up a special place for doing homework. And we were both surprised at how things have worked out. Homework has become no big deal. I can say that it's almost painless — at least for us! (Mrs. Robbins)

The next booklet I prepared was one on spelling (see Appendix K, page 95). During our first parent/teacher report card conferences it became evident that parents were confused about spelling. Some were even upset, thinking the school had abandoned the teaching of spelling altogether with the advent of whole language. I wanted something in writing that would provide us with a starting place for discussion. I hoped the booklet, entitled What about spelling?, would set aside some of their fears and help them understand how the school was addressing the spelling issue. Sent home to the parents of all children in grades three to six, the booklet proved very successful:

- So that's the story on spelling. I must admit I was concerned. The booklet helped set my mind at ease. (Mrs. March)

- I am such a terrible speller. I just couldn't imagine how Andy would learn to spell if the school wasn't teaching spelling. I think I understand what's going on now. (Mrs. Wilson)

- Thanks for the booklet about spelling. I found it interesting and it helped us think about what we could do to help. (Mr. Leah)

Booklets won't take the place of conversations with parents about various aspects of the school program — nor should they. However, they do serve to open the door to dialogue, and when a face-to-face conversation isn't possible, they may serve to diffuse a potentially volatile situation by providing parents with food for thought. If the booklets are developed communally by the staff and are in keeping with the total philosophy of the school, they also help to unify the teachers' thinking so they can speak from a common base.

Another booklet we gave to parents last year is entitled Gathering Clues. Written by Jane Power Grimm, a friend and colleague, it's intended for parents of children in the developing reader stage. They need to understand how to support their children's reading as they progress through this stage.

Although we meet with all parents to describe not only the stage of development their children are in, but also some strategies they might use to help, we find they still appreciate having the booklet on hand to refer to. It also provides a guide for parent/teacher discussions. Often teachers are tempted to give parents too many suggestions, overwhelming them with the best intentions. Some find it hard to know where to begin, or throw in too much jargon for parents to cope with. This booklet provides a framework for communication by giving parents and teachers a common ground on which to base their conversations.

There are also commercially produced pamphlets and booklets available through the International Reading Association, the National Council of Teachers of English, and an affiliate of the IRA known as RIF, Reading Is Fundamental. They cover a variety of topics: reading aloud, supporting early reading and writing, TV usage, summer reading, choosing books for children, etc.

Whether locally or commercially produced, pamphlets and booklets can provide additional information on a variety of topics and can help keep a dialogue going between parents and teachers.

Kits

Sometimes it's helpful to put together special kits. These packages of materials for parents usually consist of a collection of related booklets and pamphlets aimed at parents with children of a particular age. Kits, like the parent book bags (see page xx), provide parents with reading material of interest to them. Information sent out in this form is usually more general than that found in a single pamphlet or booklet.

Since kits are often costly to produce and time-consuming to put together, in general they aren't undertaken by individual teachers. Sometimes, however, school districts, professional associations or teacher groups initiate kit projects. Our local affiliate of the International Reading Association received a starter grant approximately five years ago when attention was first being paid in Nova Scotia to the role parents play in children's developing literacy. The grant, along with donations from local businesses, enabled the group to develop a kit to be distributed to all parents on the birth of their baby. The BABE kit (Babies and Books Early) is still given out. It contains a booklet about reading to children from birth, a booklet about nutrition, called Eating and Reading, an annotated bibliography of children's books, and a quality read-aloud book to start parents off. This kit has been highly effective in helping parents become aware of the role of storybook reading in the development of literacy.

It has also been the springboard for similar projects in the United States and elsewhere in Canada. One is a video tape/slide presentation titled Project Baby Book, produced and distributed by the Lunenburg District School Board in Nova Scotia. Additional funding has also been approved for the preparation of a follow-up kit to BABE. Developed by teachers, it has the same format as BABE, but it addresses parents of school-age children and is designed to be distributed when the children are in grade one. The READ kit (Read, Enjoy and Discover) also contains a quality children's book and bibliography.

A growing number of school districts, teacher associations and professional groups are getting involved in the preparation of quality materials for parents. If you keep your eyes open in your own area, or write to some of the groups I've mentioned for further information, you'll be able to take advantage of some of the outstanding work that has already been done. A word of caution, however. Don't be fooled into thinking that a mass-produced kit can take the place of locally produced materials. It will provide you with a resource and a model from which to design a kit that meets your own needs. And if it happens to suit your specific purposes, you'll find it a welcome addition to the materials you produce yourself.

Conclusion

As you get involved in an effort to open a two-way line of communication with parents, you can rest assured there will be others joining you. More and more teachers and administrators are realizing the need to involve parents in the learning process. You'll see conferences for parents, displays of children's work in public places, young authors' conferences and other literacy celebrations designed to give parents a good feeling of what their children can do. In Nova Scotia a network has been established through Dalhousie University's community education program to inform teachers and parents of current research findings regarding parent involvement in education and to establish a data base of related materials and programs.

If whole language teachers have learned anything over the past few years it's that, if whole language is to succeed on a wide scale, parents must understand what's going on, feel the philosophy is right for their children and know they have a rightful place in their children's education. Parents can be a very powerful support group. They can also be powerful adversaries if they feel they must protect their children from what they consider an experiment, a whim or unsound pedagogy.

Often parents feel that they can't cope with all the changes being made, that they are being left further and further behind, and this scares them. When they look at the work their children bring home and find they are just as confused as the children, that scares them too. Teachers, administrators and school districts must keep things from reaching that stage. They must build parents' confidence and trust, slowly and carefully. They must rekindle in parents the feeling that they do have a place in the education of their children and that their support and involvement is going to make a difference.

A short time ago a good friend, Ralph Peterson, gave me some very important advice. He said, "Fight only those battles you know you can win." I keep that advice in mind every time I'm about to talk with a parent. Sometimes in our zeal to explain what we're doing, or in a defensive moment, we push parents too hard, throw too much at them too fast, answer questions they had no intention of asking, or underestimate their capabilities.

Schools must begin to look at parents through different eyes if they want parents to see them differently. Whole language teachers must make an effort to take parents with them along the road to a new kind of learning. Or one day they may have to go back for those they left behind.

Appendix A: Parent survey

1. Do you consider yourself a good reader?

2. What do you like to read?

3. How often would your child see you reading?
   - ❏ every day
   - ❏ frequently
   - ❏ occasionally
   - ❏ never

4. Does your job require you to do a lot of reading?

5. Do you consider yourself a good reader? Why or why not?

6. What do you think makes a good reader?

7. Did you read before you went to school?

8. How did you learn to read?

9. Do you remember being read to as a child?

10. Would you consider your mother or father a reader?

11. How important is it to be able to read? Why?

12. How often do you read to your child?
    - ❏ every day
    - ❏ frequently
    - ❏ occasionally
    - ❏ never

13. When do you read to your child?

14. For how long?
    - ❏ 0-15 minutes
    - ❏ 15-30 minutes
    - ❏ 30-60 minutes
    - ❏ over 60 minutes

15. What are your child's favorite stories?

16. Does your child ever ask for the same story to be read over and over? If so, what do you do? Why do you suppose he [she] might want to hear the same thing so often?

Appendix B: Parent booklet

Shared language time

◆ What is it?

Shared language time is the school's counterpart of the home learning-to-speak and bedtime-story times. It's the time when we come together as a group to explore cooperatively the basic elements of language in a safe, supportive environment. It's the time when literacy strategies are modeled and the children are invited to find their own voices as language users and producers.

To help create that secure, predictable environment, our shared language time has a very definite format. During the "warm-up" phase I try to focus the children's attention on the task at hand, relax them and get their creative juices flowing. Just as bodies need stretching before any form of physical exercise, minds need to be prepared for mental activity.

I give the children a great deal of informal practice in using the patterns of written language orally, through songs, chants, Mother Goose rhymes, skipping rope rhymes and other forms of poetry. This is a relaxed, sharing time and I urge the children to take part as soon as they feel comfortable doing so. I use a wide variety of materials in each session so there'll be something of interest for everyone.

I choose materials that are predictable in nature. They have a definite structure and pattern, usually a rhyme and pronounced rhythm; but in no way is the language watered-down or controlled. Because they are quality pieces, the children are quickly able to join in with the reading.

Next is the "old favorite" segment during which we explore, in many different ways, an already familiar piece of literature, often in the form of a Big Book. When I use enlarged print the children can sit on my lap, so-to-speak, and take an active part in the story. Again I choose only quality literature with a predictable structure that allows them to join in after the first reading.

The third element of shared language time is a "new story." This is when the children experience the pleasure of discovering a brand new book. Some new stories find their way into our old favorite repertoire.

The final segment is "activity" time. The children engage in a short activity that grows naturally out of the familiar and comfortable patterns and structures they have already explored. It's not important, at this stage, that they complete each activity correctly the first time. Activities are repeated in many forms, with many pieces of literature as the springboard.

Just as children don't learn to talk all at once, they don't learn about printed language all at once. Each try moves them closer and closer to understanding the activity and how to go about accomplishing it, and I always praise them for their effort and participation without making them feel they must be perfect.

Personal writing time

◆   What is it?

Personal writing time, one half-hour daily, is when the children take an active part in writing, when they become authors themselves. They discover that they have stories, both real and imaginary, to share with others and that they can write them down using pictures, letters, invented spellings or scribbles to hold their ideas. They discover that others want to hear their stories, and they learn how to respond to someone else's writing in a positive way. They learn to share successes and to seek help with problems.

During this session they aren't concerned with letter formation or accurate spelling, although they may practice letter formation at other times during the day. Their spelling improves as they become writers; the more they write and the more they explore strategies for getting their ideas down on paper, the better it becomes. At this point I'm concerned with helping them to find their own voices, to realize that what they have to say is important and to believe that they are capable of communicating their ideas to others.

The first five minutes of the session may be a short demonstration, perhaps about how to invent spellings by putting down the sounds. Or it may be the sharing of one child's work-in-progress. Then the children get their writing folders and write for the remaining time. I circulate to each table, discussing what individuals are planning to do, hearing their stories or helping them try invented spellings.

Some of their stories will later be published; these I type and bind in book form. They are valued and read as any other book would be. At the end of the year the children take their published books home to keep and treasure with pride. They should be received with loving praise, but don't expect the children to be able to read them word-for-word. Your reading and valuing of them will be the main thing.

Independent practice time

◆   What is it?

Independent practice time is that part of the day when the children are given the opportunity to pursue investigative and literacy activities of their own choosing, using the materials available in the classroom.

The room is divided into centers: the book area, the writing area, the listening center, the discovery center, and the drama area. The children rotate in small groups from one center to the next every twenty minutes or so. The groups are reorganized every two weeks to give everyone experience working with different children. During this time I circulate and talk with groups and individuals about what they are doing, and perhaps work with individuals on specific projects or tasks. It's also during this time that I record my observations about each child.

Activity time

◆ What is it?

Activity time is an extension of independent practice time. During this portion of the day we use the facilities in a classroom that has been especially organized for this purpose. It also has centers: a sand table, a water table, a woodworking center, a discovery area, a play-house/dress-up area and a craft area. The children are given free choice of activities and can move from one area to the next whenever they wish. The only restriction is in the number of children allowed at an area. When an area is full, others must wait until someone moves. In the meantime they usually go to another activity.

Our class also has gym every day. The gym program includes a variety of equipment (balls, ropes, hoops, beanbags), large apparatus (mats, ladders, balance beam, giant ball), movement, exercise and organized games.

We have music with our music teacher for four half-hours and go to the computer room for three half-hours during each six-day cycle. On alternate days we have a computer in our classroom for the entire morning. Programs are specifically chosen to help children learn about operating the computer and to encourage problem-solving and inquiry.

Math is part of everything we do. We make graphs of what we put on our hot dogs, how we travel to school, and anything else we can think of during the course of the school year. We are constantly measuring, counting, pouring, mixing, matching, talking and writing about our discoveries. During some parts of the day we may examine a specific mathematical concept, such as patterns, more closely. At this time the children work in small groups on a specific task as I circulate to give help or encouragement. Our math program is a hands-on one where we are involved with a variety of materials to count, sort and compare in a concrete way.

Appendix C: Dialogue journal letter

Dear Parents:

I would like to enlist your help. At school I see your child involved in many interesting activities. I hear him [her] talking about what he [she] is doing at home, but I don't know what he [she] may be saying at home. As you enjoy a story together, or as he [she] writes or draws, what kinds of observations is your child making?

I'm asking you to jot down anecdotes for me in this record book, as detailed as you have the time or interest to make them. Or perhaps you have a question you'd like to ask on paper. I'd be pleased to respond. Don't worry about how you put your comments down; it's what you have to say that I'm interested in.

When you've recorded something, send the booklet to school with your child and I'll return it to you in a few days. The more contact we have with each other, the better we'll both be able to understand how your child is learning.

I realize this is an unusual request, but I hope you'll give it a try and work it into your already busy schedule!

Sincerely,

Jane Baskwill

Appendix D: Monthly newsletter

THE
B.E.A.R FACTS

NEWS FROM ROOM 5
MARCH 1987

BY THE SEA !!

Our Sea Theme is in full swing. We have the sea shell kit and the rocky shore kit from the Nova Scotia Museum. There are lots of things to handle and to look at under the magnifying glass. Please drop in and "SEA" our growing collection!

STARS OF THE SHOW

I hope those of you who were able to get to our African Show enjoyed it. I'm sure you know how hard the children worked to produce it !! Their use of space and knowing how and when to move in front of all those people required and effort in concentration not usually thought possible by five and six year olds. I hope you realize just how wonderful your children are!

Bring a Book –
Build a Dream

This is the slogan for our class' campaign to collect a children's book from each child in the Elementary School to send to a needy third world classroom. The classroom is in Basseterre, West Indies where two Nova Scotian teachers have gone to teach. They have large classes and no print materials to use. If you would like to help, please send one child's book (for any age child) to school. This can be a used book that you have in your home. The books will be collected by the children and boxed. I will take them to the Nova Scotia Reading Association Conference on April 25th where they will be put with others to be sent to the needy school. Please help build the dream of a better future for these children.

Parent Meeting:

Wednesday night, April 8th we will be holding a parent information night at the school. I will be meeting with parents from 7:00 to approximately 8:00. At this time I would like to talk a bit about how far the children have come during the year, a bit about writing and spelling and answer any questions you might have at this point. Should you wish to make an appointment to talk further about your child, we can make arrangements following the meeting or you can let me know by sending a note with your child. Often parents feel they do not want to bother the teacher with an appointment if they do not have a particular question to ask. Please do not hesitate to request a meeting – if nothing else we can swap stories about "our child".

VIDEO

The Nova Scotia Department of Education is planning to make a video of our classroom in action on Tuesday and Wednesday (Apr.28-29). There will be a camera crew, director and script consultant on the scene for the two days of filming. Following the taping I will be working along with Paulette Whitman on the commentary about what the children and I are doing. The video will be used for inservice training of teachers within this province and possibly beyond, to other provinces and the U.S. I will be sending home permission slips shortly for your signature allowing your child to take part in the project. If you have any questions, please contact me.

CALENDAR

April 8   Parent Night
April 17-20   Easter Break
April 24   Deadline for sending book
April 27-May 1 Education Week
April 28-29   Video Taping

^^^ Now that SPRING has come – so have the days of wet clothes. Please see that your child continues to wear boots during the spring months.

Appendix E: Book bag booklet

It's all in the bag

This book bag is for your family to share and enjoy for one week. Inside are books and/or cassette tapes, as well as suggested activities for you to enjoy with your child. There are thirty bags in all, so you can look forward to a new one each week.

Enclosed in each bag is a checklist of the materials it contains, so you can be sure everything comes back at the end of the week. If something is lost or damaged, please let me know so I can see to it right away. This will make it possible for all thirty bags to remain in circulation.

There is also a tape recorder available for you to borrow should there not be one in your home. If you'd like to arrange to borrow it, please let me know and I'll place your name on the schedule.

Your child will take home a book bag each Wednesday and should return it the following Wednesday. Please try to return the bags on time so each family can have a new bag every week.

I hope you and your family enjoy this program as much as I've enjoyed assembling the materials.

Suggestion: to make it easier to keep track of the materials that come in the book bag, designate a specific area of your house as the place where they are to be used (bedroom, kitchen, den, etc.).

Hints for reading with your child

Reading with your child can be a very satisfying and enjoyable experience for both of you. Just a few minutes each day, sharing a story or part of a book, can increase your child's interest in reading on his [her] own. Your encouragement at home plays a very important part in developing positive feelings about reading.

◆ What do you need in order to read to your child?

A good book and a supportive environment is all you need. Your child supplies the book, you supply the love. (A comfortable bed or chair also helps.)

◆ When should you read to your child?

You and your child should read together daily.

◆ Is there any special way you should read?

Sit comfortably with your child on your lap or close beside you so you can both see the print and the pictures. As you read, run your finger under the words. This helps your child associate the words you are reading with the print in the book. Have fun with the story. Read with expression to make it come to life. You might feel a little foolish at first, but your child will think you're a star!

Encourage your child to read along with you. Don't worry if his [her] reading doesn't quite match yours. The more familiar a story becomes, the more accurate the reading will be. The most important thing to notice is whether your child is trying to make sense of the story. In other words, even if the exact word isn't used, does the word used make sense (pup for dog, home for house) without changing the meaning of the story?

Take time to talk about the pictures and enjoy the story together. Never attempt to read a story when you're in a hurry. The experience won't be enjoyable for either of you.

◆ What books should you read to your child?

Read a variety of books, but make sure they all have good quality language. Read books you enjoy — you'll do a better job reading the ones you like — but be tolerant of your child's favorites as well. Your child may ask to hear a favorite story read over and over again. Oblige! It's important for him/her to hear stories repeated many times. And just think — if you ever lose the book, you'll be able to recite the story by heart!

Appendix F: Parent book bag suggestions

Baker, Sheena. *There's a Worm in My Apple.* Stoddart, 1985.

Parents will enjoy looking at school from the teacher's point of view. They will laugh along with you at their children and the side of the school day they don't usually see. A lighthearted book and a good companion for the Lynn Johnston books.

Boteler, Alison. *The Children's Party Handbook.* Barron, 1986; Willowisp Press, 1989.

A book of ideas for children's parties. It includes everything from costumes, decorations and recipes to games children will enjoy playing. Easy-to-follow directions.

Burtt, Kent Garland. *Smart Times.* Harper and Row, 1984.

Although written for parents of preschool children, this book continues to be helpful for older children. It's full of crafts and activities parents and children enjoy doing together.

Butler, Dorothy and Marie Clay. *Reading Begins at Home.* Heinemann, 1979, 1982.

This book helps explain the important role parents play in early literacy development. It's clearly written, with lots of examples. It's a good length and can be paired with another book along the same line, *Reading Begins at Birth.*

Butler, Dorothy. *Cushla and Her Books.* Horn, 1975, 1980.

This book, which speaks especially to parents of children with special needs, describes the story of the love and devotion of Cushla's parents and the role books played in her development. It's well written, a book all parents can appreciate.

Butler, Dorothy. *Five to Eight.* The Bodley Head, 1986.

This book picks up where *Babies Need Books* leaves off. Butler describes children's reading preferences at these ages and gives an extensive bibliography of children's books from which to choose. The main drawback is that the book is British and some of the titles listed may be difficult to find in North America. Nevertheless, it's good reading.

Canter, Lee and Marlene Canter. *Assertive Discipline for Parents.* Harper and Row, 1988.

I'm often asked for tips on how to discipline children. This book provides parents with a step-by-step approach to solving behavior problems. It helps them apply common sense, consistently.

Canter, Lee and Lee Hausner. *Homework Without Tears.* Harper and Row, 1987.

As children progess through school, homework and how to deal with it often becomes an issue. This book helps parents develop a consistent system for dealing with homework problems and helps them improve children's study skills.

Clabby, John F. and Maurice J. Elias. *Teach Your Child Decision Making.* Doubleday, 1987.

This book helps parents respond to their children's day-to-day problems in a supportive manner so the children learn to respond confidently to their own problems.

Cole, Ann, Carolyn Haas, Faith Bushnell and Betty Weinberger. *I Saw a Purple Cow.* Little, Brown, 1972.

A very popular craft book full of simple crafts children can do with a minimum of help. Materials are easy to come by and children have the satisfaction of making crafts that actually look the way they are supposed to.

Cornell, Joseph Bharat. *Sharing Nature with Children.* Ananda, 1979.

In the format of a pocket novel, this book describes the enjoyment parent and child can have when walking in the woods, collecting leaves or pine cones, or observing animals in the park or backyard. A good companion for the David Suzuki books.

Cosby, Bill. *Fatherhood*. Doubleday, 1986.

Be prepared. This one will be so popular it will get passed around to family and friends before it gets back to you! So I suggest you buy the hardcover version. Parents will easily identify with each stage described and the situtations will invoke feelings of déjà vu. A must for your collection.

Cutting, Brian. *Talk Your Way to Reading*. Shortland Publications Ltd., 1985.

This book is full of color photos and clearly written text describing to parents how children learn to talk write and read. It also gives ideas for supporting developing language skills. Highly recommended.

Doake, David B. *Reading Begins at Birth*. Scholastic, 1988.

I like to pair this book with another, such as *Reading Begins at Home,* since it's a bit more complex and at times may seem to speak more to teachers than to parents. It does, however, present parents with actual examples of children and books becoming the best of friends and demonstrates the kind of environment that influences a child's natural reading development.

Durkin, Lisa Lyons. *Parents and Kids Together*. Warner, 1986.

There are lots of activities for parents and children to do together. A favorite of parents is the section containing special cooking recipes, all easy enough to allow children to participate fully in the cooking.

Ebert, Jeanne. *What Would You Do If . . .?* Houghton Mifflin, 1985.

Parent and child are encouraged to sit together and talk about a variety of situations and how the child might handle them. It offers a starting point for discussion of personal safety. A good book to pair with *Sometimes It's Okay to Tell Secrets.*

Goodman, Kenneth. *What's Whole in Whole Language?* Scholastic, 1986; Heinemann, 1986.

Although this book is not popular with parents, I like to keep it in circulation. It describes what whole language is and what situations help to make learning easy. Because it uses the term "whole language," it allows parents to see that the concept is being researched and valued by professionals and isn't just a personal whim. It seems to be written more for teachers and this is perhaps the reason it lacks popularity with parents.

Graves, Donald and Virginia Stuart. *Write from the Start.* Dutton, 1985.

The description of an educational success story that informs parents how they can work together with teachers to improve writing instruction in school. A bit wordy.

Graves, Ruth, ed. *The RIF Guide to Encouraging Young Readers.* Doubleday, 1987.

This book offers hundreds of specially selected activities designed to engage children, from infant to 11-year-old, in the fun of exploring words and books. It's an excellent resource for parents. Highly recommended.

Gross, Jacquelyn. *Make Your Child a Lifelong Reader.* Tarcher, 1986.

A popular book with parents because it offers easy-to-understand suggestions for supporting a child's reading at home, spanning the ages from infancy to 17. I especially like chapter two, which explains many of the goals a whole language program is based on. Chapter three explains the kinds of things parents can do to have a lasting effect on a child's attitude toward reading.

Hollest, Angela, and Penelope Graine. *Children's Parties.* Piatkus, 1983.

Parents appreciate the ideas contained in this little book, especially when paired with another birthday party book. I find parents often want to purchase it for their own collection.

Hopkins, Harold. *From Talkers to Readers the Natural Way.* Ashton Scholastic, 1977.

A good little book that describes visually the development of language in young children. It's quite short and easy to read and can be paired with a more complex book like *Reading Begins at Birth.*

Johnston, Lynn. *Do They Ever Grow Up?* Meadowbrook, 1977; Stoddart, 1978.

There are many Lynn Johnston books that will appeal to parents' sense of humor, and I like to include a lighthearted bag for parents to simply enjoy. They can see themselves in many of these situations.

Lamme, Linda Leonard. *Growing Up Reading.* Acropolis, 1985.

Written especially for parents, this book offers many ideas and activities for encouraging a love of reading in children. It helps parents make reading an enjoyable family affair.

Lamme, Linda Leonard. *Growing Up Writing.* Acropolis, 1984.

Another book directed at parents, this one explains how writing skills develop naturally and provides ideas for supporting that development at home.

Lansky, Vicki. *Birthday Parties.* Bantam, 1985.

This is a very popular book, full of many common sense ideas for birthday parties. I like to pair it with another of the many good books on children's parties.

Lansky, Vicki. *Practical Parenting Tips for the School Age Years.* Bantam, 1985.

This book is so popular with parents I've had to replace it several times when it fell apart. Parents find its information about children's growth and development very helpful as their own children pass through the various stages. Although there are many books that talk about growth and development from birth to five, there aren't many that pick up from that point. Highly recommended.

Larrick, Nancy. *A Parent's Guide to Children's Reading*. Bantam, 1982; Westminster John Knox, 1983.

Parents often need help when choosing books for their children. This book offers a brief description of children's reading preferences by age and a bibliography of books from which to choose.

Lenett, Robin and Dana Barthelne. *Sometimes It's O.K. to Tell Secrets*. Harper and Row, 1985; Tor Books, 1986.

It's important for parents to sit down with their children and discuss personal safety and what to do if someone touches them in a way they don't like. This book provides a starting point for such discussions. Because it's in the parents' bag, parents can choose to not share it if they are uncomfortable.

Marzollo, Jean. *Birthday Parties for Children*. Harper, 1983.

You can never have enough birthday party ideas. This is a great little book, full of theme parties, organizational hints and things to make and do. Ideal for pairing with another party book.

Newman, Judith. *The Craft of Children's Writing*. Scholastic, 1984; Heinemann, 1985.

Although similar in format to the other books in the series, this one seems to speak more to parents. They aren't intimidated by it and can understand the writing development the author describes. I usually pair this one with *What's Whole in Whole Language?*

Oppenheim, Joanne, Barbara Brenner and Betty D. Boegehold. *Choosing Books for Kids*. Ballantine, 1986.

Another good choice for helping parents decide what books to select for their children. It has an extensive bibliography.

Sullivan, S. Adams. *The Quality Time Almanac*. Doubleday, 1986.

This book is a great find. Parents appreciate the many activities to do with their children — from crafts to science to bedtime rituals and special holiday events.

Suzuki, David. *Looking at Insects*. Stoddart, 1986; *Looking at Plants*. Stoddart, 1986.

You might want to group these titles together. They have many easy experiments for parents and children to conduct together. I usually pair these two with *Sharing Nature with Children*.

Taylor, Denny and Dorothy S. Strickland. *Family Storybook Reading*. Heinemann, 1986; Scholastic, 1986.

This book discusses with parents what happens when they share books with their children. There's an abundance of candid photos, along with many suggestions for making the most of family reading times. Parents make use of the directions for creating their own family storybooks.

Trelease, Jim. *The Read-Aloud Handbook*. Penguin, 1985.

A highly popular and easy read, this book presents a good case for reading aloud to children of all ages. The section on TV watching also makes quite an impression.

Van Manen, Max. *The Tone of Teaching*. Scholastic, 1985; Heinemann, 1985.

This book gives parents a feeling for what a whole language classroom is like. It's a very sensitive and well written book that parents can identify with. I pair it with *What's Whole in Whole Language?* or *The Craft of Children's Writing*.

Appendix G: Parent book bag letter

Dear Parents:

Don't let the title Fatherhood fool you. Bill Cosby is talking to mothers, fathers, aunts and grandmothers! You'll find his stories funny and easy reading, but you'll be able to see the truth in each situation.

My favorite piece is titled "The First Parent Had Trouble, Too", which you'll find on page 64. If you don't have time to read anything else, make time to read that one. I think you'll find it enjoyable. Who knows, after reading page 64 you might want to read some more.

I've placed a card in the back of the book. If you'd like to, please write down your opinions. Did you like the book? Did you have a favorite part? If so, which one? You needn't write more than a few words.

Happy reading!

Sincerely,

Jane Baskwill

Appendix H: Parent interview questions

1. How often do you read to your child? If you don't read to him [her], who does? What kinds of stories do you usually read? Where? When?

2. How do you keep your child's interest when you read?

3. Does your child usually ask to be read to?

4. When you read to your child what do your older/younger children do?

5. Does your child ever read to himself [herself]? What does he [she] do?

6. How would you describe your child's reading? How do you feel you support his [her] literacy learning at home?

7. What do you feel will help your child most at this time? How can you help? How is that different from my role as a teacher?

8. What do you think of our weekly book bag program? How do you use the books?

9. How do you feel about the book bag program for parents? About our newsletters? meetings? slide show? (etc.)

Appendix I: Lunch box launchers

Anno, Mitsumasa. *Anno's Counting Book.* Crowell, 1977.

Anno, Mitsumasa. *Anno's Counting House.* Putnam, 1982

Anno, Mitsumasa. *Anno's Hat Tricks.* Putnam, 1985

Anno, Mitsumasa. *Anno's Math Games.* Putnam, 1987.

Anno, Mitsumasa. *Anno's Mysterious Multiplying Jar.* Putnam, 1983

Anno, Mitsumasa. *Anno's Sundial.* Putnam, 1987

Baum, Joseph and Arlene. *Opt: an illusionary tale.* Penguin, 1987.

Berger, Melvin. *Simple Science Says: Take One Balloon,* Scholastic, 1988.

Berger, Melvin. *Simple Science Says: Take One Mirror.* Scholastic, 1989.

Carson, Mary Stetten. *The Scientific Kid.* Fitzhenry and Whiteside, 1989; Harper and Row, 1989.

Francis, Neil. *Super Flyers.* Kids Can, 1988.

Handford, Martin. *Where's Waldo?* Little Brown.

Hoban, Tana. *Count and See.* Macmillan, 1972.

Hoban, Tana. *Look! Look! Look!* Morrow, 1988.

Hoban, Tana. *Push-Pull, Empty-Full.* Macmillan, 1972.

Hutchins, Pat. *Changes Changes.* Macmillan, 1971.

Hutchins, Pat. *Clocks and More Clocks.* Macmillan, 1970.

Hutchins, Pat. *Rosie's Walk.* Macmillan, 1968.

Mori, Tvyosi. *Socrates and the Three Little Pigs.* Putnam, 1986

Ontario Science Centre. *Foodworks.* Kids Can, 1986.

Ontario Science Centre. *Have Fun With Magnifying.* Kids Can, 1987.

Ontario Science Centre. *How Sport Works.* Kids Can, 1988.

Ontario Science Centre. *Scienceworks.* Kids Can Press, 1984.

Oxenbury, Helen. *Numbers of Things.* Delacorte, 1967.

Ripley, Catherine, ed. *Kitchen Fun.* Greey de Pencier, 1988.

Royal Ontario Museum. *Discover: mysteries of the past and present*. Kids Can, 1989.

Smithsonian Institute. *More Science Activities*. Galison Books, 1988.

Spier, Peter. *Fast-Slow, High-Low*. Doubleday, 1972.

Stein, Sarah. *The Science Book*. Workman, 1980.

Suzuki, David. *Looking at Insects*. Stoddart, 1986.

Suzuki, David. *Looking at Plants*. Stoddart, 1985.

Suzuki, David. *Looking at the Body*. Stoddart, 1987.

Suzuki, David. *Looking at the Environment*. Stoddart, 1989.

Testa, Fulvio. *If You Look Around You*. Dial, 1983.

Thomas, Lyn. *What's It*. Greey de Pencier. 1988.

Appendix J: Activity calendar

October

1 Thursday

2 Friday

3 Saturday

4 Sunday

5 Monday

6 Tuesday

7 Wednesday

8 Thursday

9 Friday

10 Saturday

11 Sunday

12 Monday

13 Tuesday

14 Wednesday

15 Thursday

16 Friday

17 Saturday

18 Sunday

19 Monday

20 Tuesday

21 Wednesday

22 Thursday

23 Friday

24 Saturday

25 Sunday

26 Monday

27 Tuesday

28 Wednesday

29 Thursday

30 Wednesday

31 Thursday

Peter, Peter, pumpkin eater,

Had a wife and couldn't keep her;

Put her in a pumpkin shell

And there he kept her very well.

Monster Catalogue

Make a catalogue of all the different Halloween creatures you might expect to see on Halloween night. Draw a picture of each one and give it a name. Tell something about its special powers. Design a cover and fasten your pages together with staples or yarn. When your book is finished you might like to share it with a friend. The creatures in your book can also become characters in a Halloween story you make up.

Clifford's Halloween Norman Bridwell
Meg and Mog Helen Nicoll
The Biggest Pumpkin Ever Steven Kroll
Harry And The Terrible Whatzit Dick Gackenback

Halloween Finger Puppets

box of facial tissues   glue
paper   small elastic or thread
crayons or markers†

Ghost: Fold tissue over. Hold in place with elastic or thread. Draw eyes and mouth.
Jack-o-lantern: Cut jack-o-lantern shape and colour. Make loop to fit on finger. Glue to back of jack-o-lantern.

Spooky Cupcakes

cupcakes - already cooled
frosting - assorted colours
chocolate chips, raisins, small candies (for eyes, noses, mouths, etc.)
licorice strips (whiskers)
Assemble into various Halloween characters: black cats, jack-o-lanterns, ghosts, etc.)

Book and Character Costumes

Help your child try something different this Halloween. Dress up as a favourite storybook character — or the book itself.

How can you make a paper clip move without touching it?

1 paper clip or safety pin
1 magnet
1 piece of paper

Put the paper clip or safety pin on the paper. Hold the paper with one hand and move the magnet under the paper with the other. The paper clip will move wherever the magnet moves.

Appendix K: What about spelling?

Spelling is a developmental process. Spelling develops as children try new strategies and refine or change what they used to believe to be true in light of new information. It develops when children have the chance to use what they know about how language works in order to predict, confirm, integrate or establish relationships among words they want to write.

Spelling is not simply memorizing a list of words. We all know someone who received 100% on weekly spelling tests but when writing letters, reports or term papers lost credit because of numerous spelling errors. Teachers and parents have known for a long time that there's often little carryover from weekly lists to daily writing. If we are to improve children's spelling, we must include more than spelling lists in their program. We must give them lots of opportunities to practice the process of spelling, as we do when we involve them in a quality writing program. Although lists might be part of that program, much more has to be involved as well. It's our hope that this pamphlet will help you better understand our spelling program.

What good spellers do

Although good spellers needn't demonstrate all the following skills, they usually demonstrate some of them. They:

- have an interest in words;

- write a lot;

- read a lot (which gives them a large vocabulary);

- aren't afraid to make spelling predictions based on their knowledge of other words;

- visualize the word (they sense when it looks right);

- have a feel for the word (they sense when it feels right as they write it);

- have their own spelling aids for difficult words (they remember the word here is in the word there, for example);

- recognize when a word is spelled incorrectly and know where to go for the correct word;

- have a good memory;

- see relationships among words and are able to categorize words with similar spellings (if they can spell discover, they can spell rediscover, discovery and so on);

- see generalizations (they know when specific spelling rules apply).

How our school teaches spelling

Our spelling program strives to help children:

- develop a respect for standard spelling and a desire to achieve it when they write;

- realize that spelling is a process that involves using a variety of clues to predict and confirm the spelling of a word;

- become curious about the structure and meanings of words.

In order to achieve this we:

- teach spelling as part of the whole curriculum, capitalizing on opportunities to have the children write and spell in situations other than the spelling lesson — in math, science, social studies and so on;

- have the children write frequently, since they predict and refine spelling by using skills they acquire when they write labels, letters, posters, stories, reports, signs, etc.;

- encourage the children to use functional (invented) spelling for words they may not have learned to spell conventionally (this way they think about how the word might be spelled, based on their knowledge of other words, while still getting their ideas down intact, knowing they can correct the spelling at a later time);

- adjust our expectations of correctness to fit the child's level of development, making allowances for inexperience and mistakes but expecting the child, without feeling the need to be perfect all the time, to recognize that there are times when it's necessary;

- respond to children's writing in ways that help them discover more about spelling (for instance, we make word study a game but teach spelling skills and strategies at the same time);

- help young writers develop a positive attitude toward spelling.

How you can help your child at home

Your understanding and support now are just as critical as they were when your child learned to walk, talk and read. Here's what you can do to help at home:

- Play word games with your child: Scrabble, crossword puzzles, Spill 'n Spell, word lotto, etc. When children need to think about the details of words their spelling skills and knowledge of words are extended.

- Find ways for your child to use writing for a real purpose: letters to friends and relatives, pen pals, sending for free materials, messages, cards, shopping lists, stories and poems as gifts for family members, etc. By writing for a real purpose, children discover the importance and relevance of correct spelling.

◆ Draw your child's attention to a variety of print forms: greeting cards, advertisements, magazines, newspapers, TV guides, comics, etc. Children discover many new words this way.

◆ Talk frequently with your child about what he or she is interested in or doing, where he or she is going, etc. Children learn new words by hearing others use them. It's hard to spell a word whose meaning you don't know.

◆ Be supportive of your child's spelling attempts, encouraging best guesses. Point out when words are spelled like other familiar words or when they have beginnings or endings tacked on. You can ask older children to circle words they think they've misspelled. Don't expect children to check long lists all at once. Decide on the number to be fixed and talk about how to find the standard spellings.

◆ Your child's spelling will develop over time. Be patient and supportive, as you always have been, and your child will become a better speller — one who not only gets the words right on a spelling test but who is able to spell more consistently and accurately for all kinds of writing tasks.

Selected references

Journal articles

Bangs DeJesus, Susan E. "Literacy and the home: a true story." *Language Arts.* 1985, 62, #8, 845-847.

Brailsford, Anne. "Kindergarten readers in progress." *Reading-Canada-Lecture.* 1986, 4, #2, 113-124.

Brause, Reta S. and John S. Mayher. "Learning through teaching: language at home and in school." *Language Arts.* 1985, 62, #8, 870-875.

Burke, Carolyn. "Parenting, teaching, and learning as a collaborative venture." *Language Arts.* 1985, 62, #8, 836-843.

Cassidy, Jack and Carol Vukelich. "Survival reading for parents and kids: a parent education program." *Reading Teacher.* 1978, 31, #6, 638-641.

Doake, David B. "Book experiences and emergent reading behavior in preschool children." Unpublished doctoral disertation, University of Alberta, 1981.

Durkin, Dolores. "Early readers-reflections after six years of research." *Reading Teacher.* 1964, 18, 3-7.

Esworthy, Helen Feaga. "Parents attend reading clinic, too." *Reading Teacher.* 1979, 32, #7, 831-834.

Flood, James. "Parental styles in reading episodes with young children." *Reading Teacher.* 1977, 30, #8, 864-867.

Foulks, Patricia. "How early should language development and pre-reading experiences be started?" *Elementary English*. 1974, 42, 310-315.

Gates, Arthur. "Basal principals in reading readiness testing." *Teacher's College Record*. 1939, 40, 495-506.

Granowsky, Alvin, Frances R. Middleton and Janice H. Mumford. "Parents as partners in education." *Reading Teacher*. 1979, 32, #7, 826-830.

Greaney, Vincent. "Parental influences on reading." *Reading Teacher*. 1986, 39, #8, 813-818.

Holbrook, Hilary Taylor. "Teachers working with parents." *Language Arts*. 1985, 62, #8, 897-901.

Hoskisson, Kenneth. "Learning to read naturally." *Language Arts*. 1979, 56, #5, 489-494.

Lamme, Linda Leonard and Athol B. Packer. "Bookreading behaviors of infants." *Reading Teacher*. 1986, 39, #6, 504-509.

Lautenschlager, John and Karl V. Hertz. "Inexpensive, worthwhile, educational — parents reading to children." *Reading Teacher*. 1984, 38, #1, 18-20.

Manning, Maryann and Gary Manning. "Early readers and non-readers from low socioeconomic environments: What their parents report." *Reading Teacher*. 1984, 38, #1, 32-34.

Martinez, Miriam and William H. Teale. "The ins and outs of a kindergarten writing program." *Reading Teacher*. 1987, 40, #4, 444-451.

Mayfield, Margie I. "Parents, children and reading: helping Canadian Native Indian parents of preschoolers." *Reading Teacher*. 1985, 39, #3, 301-305.

Nicholson, Tom. "Why we need to talk to parents about reading." *Reading Teacher*. 1980, 34, #1, 19-21.

Pikulski, John J. "Parents can aid reading growth." *Elementary English*. 1974, 51, 896-897.

Quisenberry, Lynn K., Candace Blakemore and Claudia A. Warren. "Involving parents in reading: an annotated bibliography." *Reading Teacher*. 1977, 31, #1, 34-39.

Taylor, Denny. "The family and the development of literacy skills and values." *Journal of Research in Reading.* 1981, 4, #2, 92-103.

Taylor, Denny. "Translating children's everyday uses of print into classroom practice." *Language Arts.* 1986, 59, #6, 546-549.

Teale, William H. "Parents reading to their children: what we know and need to know." *Language Arts.* 1981, 58, #8, 902-911.

Teale, William H. "Positive environments for learning to read: what studies of early readers tell us." *Language Arts.* 1978, 55, #5, 922-932.

Tway, Eileen. "Home-school links." *Language Arts.* 1985, 62, #8, 889-895.

Vukelich, Carol. "Parents are teachers: a beginning reading program." *Reading Teacher.* 1978, 31, #5, 524-527.

Weeks, Thelma. "Early reading development as language development." *Language Arts.* 1979, 56, #5, 515-521.

Weisner, Margaret. "Parental responsibility in the teaching of reading." *Young Children.* 1964, 19, 225-230.

Books

Atwell, Nancie. *In the Middle.* Portsmouth: Boynton/Cook, 1987.

Baskwill, Jane and Paulette Whitman. *Whole Language Sourcebook.* Toronto: Scholastic-TAB Publications, 1986.

Bissex, Glinda L. *Gyns at Wrk: A Child Learns to Write and Read.* Cambridge: Harvard University Press. 1980.

Busching, Beverly A. and Judith I. Schwartz. *Integrating the Language Arts in the Elementary School.* Urbana: NCTE, 1983.

Butler, Dorothy. *Cushla and Her Books.* London: Hodder and Stoughton, 1979.

Clark, Margaret M. *Young Fluent Readers.* London: Heinemann Educational Books, 1976.

Durkin, Dolores. *Children Who Read Early.* New York: Teacher's College Press, 1966.

Ferreiro, Emilia and Ana Teberosky. *Literacy Before Schooling.* Portsmouth: Heinemann Educational Books, 1982.

Hansen, Jane, Thomas Newkirk and Donald Graves. *Breaking Ground: Teachers Relate Reading and Writing in the Elementary School.* Portsmouth: Heinemann Educational Books, 1985.

Harste, Jerome C., Virginia Woodward and Carolyn Burke. *Language Stories and Literacy Lessons.* Portsmouth: Heinemann Educational Books, 1984.

Holdaway, Don. *The Foundations of Literacy.* Sydney: Ashton Scholastic, 1979.

Jager, Angela and M. Trike Smith-Burke. *Observing the Language Learner.* Urbana: IRA/NCTE, 1985.

Meek, Margaret. *Learning to Read.* London: The Bodley Head, 1982; Portsmouth: Heinemann Educational Books, 1985.

Newkirk, Thomas and Nancie Atwell. *Understanding Writing.* Portsmouth: Heinemann Educational Books, 1986.

Newman, Judith. *The Craft of Children's Writing.* Toronto: Scholastic-TAB Publications, 1984; Portsmouth: Heinemann Educational Books, 1985.

Newman, Judith M. *Whole Language: Theory in Use.* Portsmouth: Heinemann Educational Books, 1985.

Taylor, Denny. *Family Literacy.* Portsmouth: Heinemann Educational Books, 1983.

Tizard, Barbara and Martin Hughes. *Young Children Learning.* London: Fontana, 1984; Cambridge: Harvard University Press, 1985.

Tovey, Duane R. and James E. Kerber. *Roles in Literacy Learning.* Newark: IRA, 1986.

Wells, Gordon. *The Meaning Makers: Children Learning Language and Using Language to Learn.* Portsmouth: Heinemann Educational Books, 1986.